Scenery an

The Teifi:
Scenery and Antiquities of a Welsh River

by

Richard J. Colyer

Gomer Press
1987

First impression - 1987

ISBN 0 86383 435 3

© Richard J. Colyer

Printed by
J. D. Lewis & Sons Ltd.
Gomer Press, Llandysul, Dyfed

To

M.J.S.C.

with love and gratitude

Contents

Preface

This book is born of several weeks walking along the banks of the River Teifi in the eminently forgettable wet summer of 1985. Like the river, the book is modest in scale and has two simple objectives, namely those of providing an historical guide for visitors to the Teifi area and of increasing the awareness of residents and local historians of the tremendous richness of the history and traditions of the river and its immediate locality. In the hope that local antiquaries, students and school pupils will pursue in detail some of the points which I have sketched in outline, I have provided footnotes and a short bibliography. Both, however, have been reduced to an absolute minimum and "general" works on the history, geography and topography of Wales have not been included.

Anyone writing about the history of Wales, however modest the scope of their work, must acknowledge the invaluable assistance of the staffs of the National Library of Wales and the National Monuments Record (Wales), both located in Aberystwyth. These apart, I am indebted for helpful comments and criticism to Dr. C. S. Briggs of the Royal Commission on Ancient Monuments and Professor I. G. Jones, Dr. G. Jenkins, Mr. J. B. Smith and Mr. D. F. P. Gwynne of the University College of Wales, Aberystwyth. My atrocious handwriting has been transformed into impeccable typescript by Mrs. D. Thomas and Mr. N. D. H. Chapman, while Mr. J. J. Wells was responsible for producing the maps. The photographs on pages 33, 48, 53, 59 and 68 appear by courtesy of the National Library of Wales while all remaining illustrations, mistakes, mis-spellings, and factual and grammatical errors are entirely my own. Map reference in this volume are based upon the following Ordnance Survey Sheets: Chapters I and II, 1: 63360 (140); Chapters III to V, 1: 50,000 (145).

RICHARD J. COLYER
24 May, 1986

Introduction

Rivers have always exercised a profound influence upon the imaginations of men. The lively dance of a mountain stream in full spate, the sluggish timelessness of a mature river flowing through low-lying meadows, the dark mystery of the deep pool and the desolate melancholy of salt-flats on an estuary have long been a source of inspiration to poets and painters alike. Some have responded to the sheer beauty of rivers; their light, colour and restless movement, while others have seen the flow of water as a powerful metaphor for the passage of time or the pointlessness of struggling against the inevitable. Matthew Arnold saw man as a wanderer "on the breast of the river of Time" and Tennyson, in that wonderful poem "The Princess", extended the metaphor further:

"Ask me no more: thy fate and mine are sealed:
I strove against the stream and all in vain:
Let the great river take me to the main:
No more, dear love, for at a touch I yield;
Ask me no more.'

To T. S. Eliot, the brown god of the river, "sullen, untamed and intractable" is an untrustworthy, implacable foe:

"Keeping his seasons and rages, destroyer, reminder
Of what men choose to forget. Unhonoured,
  unpropitiated
By worshippers of the machine, but waiting,
  watching and waiting . . ."

The image of the river as a powerful and malignant destructive force is common in European literature. Bridges, buildings and the bloated bodies of cattle, sheep, men and women are swept away time and again by rivers. Ophelia met her end in the "weeping brook" and the shadow of the Floss hung menacingly over George Eliot's Tulliver family until it finally claimed the lives of Tom and Maggie. And here is a bitter irony; for without the Floss there would have been no Dorlcote Mill for the children to live out their cloudless early days.

Hoary with years and powered by the energetic river, Dorlcote Mill provided a livelihood for generations of Tullivers. So too the restless flow of rivers generated a source of income for tradesmen of all descriptions before they were rendered redundant by the relentless advance of steam. Corn grinders, cloth weavers, copper and iron smelters all relied upon the motive power of running water so that the local river and its tributaries became inextricably linked with the economy of the area. To the riverside came the farmer's cart, the brewer's dray, the cloth merchant with his train of packhorses and the blacksmith's boy with his handcart. The river was a vital element in their daily lives. To be sure, it was potentially dangerous and, in certain seasons, a menacing threat, but yet in the normal runs of events it was a vital artery along which flowed the power to fuel commercial activity.

And it was more besides. Throughout Britain and the rest of Europe rivers have formed cultural, ethnic and linguistic boundaries; they have provided channels of communication and, perhaps most important of all, they have been defensive barriers for embattled populations nervously watching their frustrated aggressors. Often in the history of war armies and whole populations have been saved from destruction by the presence of a deep and rapidly-flowing river.

If the banks of many British rivers have resounded to the clang of swords and the ring of chain mail, they have more commonly echoed the "swish" of fishing lines (and the elaborate, if harmless fabrications of those who wield them!). Over a quiet day's fishing, deals have been clinched, territorial disputes restored and family differences settled. Harassed tycoons with dangerously high blood pressures have turned for solace to the salmon of the Tweed and Wye and many an angry shop steward has reflected on the week's negotiations as he cast a line into the quiet waters of the Nene or Ouse. River banks are excellent places for solitary contemplation. They provide havens for henpecked husbands, chastised wives, frustrated lovers and rejected mistresses. And ultimately, for those with problems which appear insoluble, the river offers a final, if somewhat drastic solution . . .

Britain has no great rivers. There are no vast Mississippis, no shape-shifting, monsoon-fed flows like those of India or Bangladesh and few which compete with the sheer drama of the rock-enclosed torrents of the European Alps. Our rivers rarely occupy a central or pivotal role in folk legend or origin-myths unlike many in Europe and Asia. The Rhine flows serenely through the bloodstained pages of The *Nibelungenlied* and through Wagner's gigantic, muscle-bound distortion of that tale; the Danube and the Vltava feature prominently in Central European folk tradition while a Russian folk tale without some reference to the Volga is almost unthinkable. True, rivers appear time and again in our music, literature and painting but have never become deeply ingrained in the national consciousness. Like so much of our landscape they are modest in scale; undramatic, understated and without pretension. Like the stream in Constable's "Haywain", the unassuming British river conveys an image of permanence, of stability, of "olde England"; timeless and changeless. Perhaps because they are, by world standards, trivial affairs, some British painters have often been tempted to imbue their rivers with a drama and monumental quality which they rarely possess. The glowering skies and threatening mountains in Paul Sandy Munn's painting of Tanybwlch (Gwynedd), completed in 1802, lend to the nearby river a sinister and rather awesome quality far removed from reality. In similar vein, John "Warwick" Smith, who produced so many rich and sonorous watercolours of Welsh subjects in the late 18th century, accentuated the cascades of the waterfall at Rhaeadr-y-wennol in a highly romantic and illusory manner. But such people, teetering on the brink of Romanticism and profoundly influenced by grandiose Alpine scenery, were generally in the minority and as a rule the river in British art becomes largely incidental to associated human activity. Thus rivers tend to serve as convenient boundaries to gentlemens' parks, settings for rural frolics, backgrounds to paintings of favourite dogs, and occasionally, like Millais' rather fey portrait of Ruskin, backcloths to images of famous men.

Unassuming though most of them are, the channels and vales created by British rivers display marvellous diversity in size, shape and setting. And this is as much the case in Wales as in other parts of the kingdom. A casual glance at almost any Ordnance Survey sheet reveals a bewildering variety of waterflows dignified with the prefix *afon,* many of them being little more than streams negotiable by an active man in a single leap. Yet these diminutive watercourses, rattling busily through their stony beds on the short journey towards the sea, can be every bit as fascinating as their grander brethren. The distinguished rivers of the east and south, like the Wye, the Severn, the Dee and the Usk, possess a dignity and majesty that has excited generations of photographers and tourists. By comparison, the waters of the west have been overlooked, appreciation of their more subtle attributes being generally limited to local people and connoisseurs. But it is the very modesty of their scale and length which lends charm to streams such as the Ystwyth, the Aeron, the Rheidol and the subject of this essay, the River Teifi.

Today, few sea-going vessels sail on the tide from the mouth of the Teifi; the many and various small industries previously adorning its lower reaches have long since disappeared; slate and stone quarries have been abandoned, fish weirs destroyed and mill wheels silenced. Yet the river flows on, following much the same course as it did when the fabulous Cunedda swept down into Dyfed and legendary figures in *The Mabinogion* hunted alongside its banks. And what a river it is! Rising only 16 miles from the sea and travelling a mere 70 miles, it edges its way through some of the loveliest countryside in Britain, undergoing a gradual metamorphosis from mountain stream to mature river. In the process it passes quiet market towns and timeless farms, gentrified parks and stern hill forts, mysterious peat bogs and arcadian meadows, before finally flowing through a series of dramatically-incised gorges to meet the sea at the old port of Cardigan. A good athlete would have little difficulty in running the course of the Teifi in two days. To those inclined to the more civilised business of gentle walking, with frequent interruptions for refreshment and contemplation, four or five days will be sufficient. This little book has been compiled with such travellers in mind and if the following description of the history, antiquities and scenery of Teifiside enhance their enjoyment of this lovely river and its surrounding countryside, it will have served some purpose.

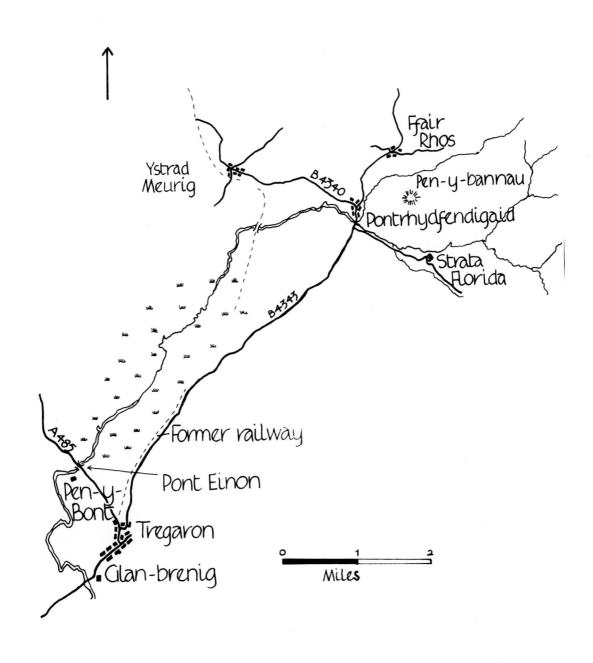

Ffair Rhos

Ystrad Meurig

B 4340

Pen-y-bannau

Pontrhydfendigaid

Strata Florida

B 4343

A 485

Former railway

Pont Einon

Pen-y-Bont

Tregaron

Glan-brenig

0   1   2

Miles

CHAPTER ONE

The Upper Reaches;
Teifi Pools to Tregaron

The Cardiganshire town of Tregaron seems to rest incongruously on the edge of two worlds. Westwards lie the undulating, well wooded pasturelands of the coastal parishes; gentle, hospitable and prosperous, a landscape of homely farms and scattered villages embraced by the broad expanse of Cardigan Bay. To the east, in dramatic contrast, stretches remote high country of wind and moorgrass, rushes and rocks. This is a wet land where dark peat bogs alternate with outcrops of bare rock, where wind and cloud can easily disorientate the unwary traveller, and where whitening sheep skeletons serve as grisly reminders that in this environment livestock subsist at the boundaries of survival. Yet even here, Art has, to some extent at least, laid a restraining hand on Nature, as witness the occasional bright green patch of "improved" grazing, the dark blotch of a forest of conifers, the steel-framed gate, and the rusty galvanised sheet.

On the edge of this land, some five miles to the north-east of Tregaron, and seemingly imprisoned in the rock-strewn, barren uplands, is a group of deep, brown lakes. These are the Teifi pools, famed in medieval times for the excellence of their trout and eels and the fact that one of them, at least, was believed to be unfathomable. From the largest of these, Llyn Teifi, the infant river cascades lazily towards the meadows by the ruins of the Abbey of Strata Florida hundreds of feet below. Today the river pursues a course through open grassland where cast-off bottles and beer cans remind us of the less acceptable face of tourism, and redundant bedframes lodged uneasily into tumble-down stone walls of the decline in a vital rural craft. But it was not always so. When the Cistercian monks came to the area, seeking that remoteness and isolation so essential to the practice of their devotions, the slopes below Llyn Teifi were densely clad with woods of oak and birch which millennia

The countryside around Teifi Pools

The infant Teifi

Council and other well-meaning bodies. If farmers are not prepared to fence their woodlands against these most destructive of animals, there is a distinct likelihood that no natural woodland will remain for the delectation of their grandchildren[2].

On its descent from the mountain the Teifi receives tiny tributaries and by the time it runs through the oak copse immediately above the abbey ruins it begins to bear some resemblance to a river, flowing gently between banks lined with alder, willow and ash. Here seven centuries ago, the Cistercian monks may well have wandered after a hard day's toil on one of their several granges, thinking, perhaps of their princely patron Rhys ap Gruffudd whose generosity provided them with the means to build one of the largest and most beautiful monastic buildings of West Wales. Some may have reflected upon the enormous task of conveying stone from Somerset to the little port of Aber-arth and subsequently overland to the abbey site, others on the hard graft expended in developing their granges, farms, gardens and orchards and others yet upon the painstaking labour of illuminating manuscripts. Thanks to the efforts of these men this great abbey in this remote corner of Cardiganshire became a major cultural and economic centre, surviving lightning, fire, military activity and the changing fortunes of the medieval economic climate[3]. With encouragement from the Crown the monks became major exporters of wool and there are indications that the native peasantry were so impressed by the success of the sheep-orientated monastic granges that they became flockmasters themselves. Thus, the early thirteenth century witnessed a gradual change in local farming practice whereby sheep production increased in importance in an economy previously dominated by cattle.

Visitors to the great fairs of nearby Ffair-rhos and Ystradmeurig, supposedly established by the monks to market their farm products and those of the local peasantry, often combined business with devotional duties by making a pilgrimage to the abbey[4]. In so doing they would be joined by other pilgrims, on their way perhaps to St. Davids, or even to Rome itself[5]. If it meant a

before had provided sustenance for early man. Within three centuries of the completion of the great cruciform abbey the woodlands had succumbed to the axe. Of those trees not cleared by the monks themselves, some were felled under the order of successive Anglo-Norman kings anxious to deny their Welsh adversaries cover for guerilla operations, and others were ruthlessly chopped down to provide charcoal for lead smelting. So complete had the process been that in 1536 when Henry VIII's servant, John Leland, surveyed Strata Florida prior to the Dissolution, his horse carried him through a substantially deforested landscape. Outlining the various reasons for the disappearance of the woodlands, Leland soberly observed that once the trees had been removed, ". . . the gottys hath so bitten the young spring that it never grew but lyke shrubbes"[1] Over four and a half centuries Leland's implied plea for woodland regeneration rings true today. The large herds of "gottys" have long since disappeared, yet sheep continue to forage voraciously through many of Cardiganshire's remaining tracts of deciduous woodland despite the remonstrations of the Nature Conservancy diversion from a more direct route, a visit to Strata Florida was always reckoned worthwhile by the devout for here was housed the fabulous relic known to later ages as the "Nanteos Cup". Claimed by some to be a fragment of the true Cross and by others the chalice used at the Last Supper, the well-worn wooden cup apparently possessed miraculous healing properties and its use was eagerly sought by the scrofulous, the maimed and the otherwise infirm. Rich and poor alike flocked to the abbey in the hope of relief from their various afflictions (and in the certain knowledge that the cup's custodians would relieve them of at least some of the contents of their pockets in return for the privilege of sipping from the precious relic).

For the best part of two centuries the abbey and its incumbents flourished, their wealth growing as their territories expanded. However, during the rebellion of Owain Glyndŵr in the early 15th century, the monks played unwilling hosts to a garrison of royal troops with unfortunate consequences for the fabric of the buildings.

Later, it seems, the monks quarrelled among themselves and as the demesne lands and granges became less profitable they were let out to lay tenants. Such was the process of decline that on the eve of the Dissolution Strata Florida supported a mere six monks and an abbot on a rental income of £150. In the unseemly struggle for monastic lands following Henry VIII's rift with Rome, Strata Florida and its far-flung territories came briefly into the hands of the earls of Essex before being sold to a member of the Stedman family who built the rather distinguished farmhouse still standing close to the abbey ruins. With the marriage of a later Stedman daughter to the heir of the powerful Powell family of Nanteos near Aberystwyth, the property became part of the Nanteos inheritance, as did the famous cup which had happily escaped the clutches of Edward VI's zealous "anti-relic" commissioners[6].

Originally, the abbey of Strata Florida stood in magnificent isolation, its great east window looking out onto empty hills. Today it is hem-

Strata Florida: the Abbey ruins

17

Strata Florida: the Abbey ruins

med in on the northern side by a large cemetery where the dead rest quietly in well-regimented rows, awaiting the last trump under sombre memorials of black marble. Overshadowing them all is an astonishing monolith commemorating the life of that great philanthropist and patron of Welsh culture, Sir David James. In contrast to this obtrusive and rather ostentatious obelisk, the reputed resting place of Dafydd ap Gwilym (fl. 1340–1370), the greatest Welsh poet of his own and subsequent ages, is marked by a simple plaque overshadowed by an ancient yew tree. To the south of the cemetery, decomposing in peace beneath plain weathered slabs, lie the dead monks of the abbey along with many of those Welsh lordlings whose warlike adventures feature so prominently in the annals of medieval Cardiganshire. Although their graves are not identified, we know several of their names from that remarkable document, *Brut y Tywysogyon* which chronicles the bloodstained history of the princes of medieval Wales. Thus Gruffydd ap Rhys, Prince of Deheubarth

Graveyard: Strata Florida

18

(d. 1137) is buried not far from Maelgwyn ap Rhys (d. 1230), a turbulent and aggressive character who spent a good deal of his time fighting with his brother for control of the ancestral territories. Owain ap Gruffydd ap Rhys (d. 1235) rests close by as do many besides, the more fortunate dying in their beds, others gasping out their last agonised breath on the field of battle[7].

A mile or so down river from the abbey stands the village of Pontrhydfendigaid, where much-modernised cottages bedecked with the slogans of ecologically-conscious outsiders nestle slightly uneasily alongside the homes of local people. Bont, as the place is affectionately known, is not perhaps the most attractive of Welsh villages, but if it lacks immediate aesthetic appeal, it is nevertheless an interesting and rewarding place for the casual wanderer. For whatever reason, be it the presence of increasing numbers of expatriot English, the growth of tourism, or the stimulus presently being given to

Pontrhydfendigaid Bridge

private initiative, some local and non-local crafts have managed to survive in Pontrhydfendigaid as, indeed, they have in other villages in this part of west Wales. Not far from the "Heddle" tea rooms, advertising gemstones in addition to tea, cakes, bed and breakfast, the smell of wet clay and the sound of craftsmen at work draw one inexorably to the local pottery where Messrs Edwards, Morgan and Bulman produce fine handthrown and decorated stoneware. A century ago, of course, Pontrhydfendigaid and kindred villages were the nerve-centres of the rural economy boasting numerous craftsmen producing a whole range of goods for local consumption by cottage and farm. The discovery of a nearby chalybeate spring in the late 19th century must have dramatically affected both craftsmen and other residents. What a windfall of good fortune would follow if Pontrhydfendigaid were to become a second Llandrindod Wells; a Welsh Matlock, a Cardiganshire Buxton! But, as the antiquary Horsfall-Turner ruefully admitted, "The chalybeate spring, although it contain ten grains of solid per gallon, has not yet produced the rush of the health and pleasure seeker to Bont . . ."[8]. So the village slumbered on into the twentieth century.

For more than a thousand years lead had been mined and smelted in west Cardiganshire and it is just possible that concern with lead pollution contributed to the failure of the chalybeate spring project. If the physiological basis to lead poisoning was only barely understood, people were nevertheless just as alive to the potential dangers of high levels of lead in water supplies as they are today. Locally the problem was highlighted in 1848 by an almost surreal event which took place in a field adjoining the Talbot Hotel in Tregaron; namely the burying of an elephant! This unhappy animal, the property of a travelling circus, had apparently died from lead poisoning, a fact which so concentrated local minds that petitions were dispatched to London in the hope that the authorities would make some effort to enforce pollution control measures on mining contractors. Local pressure, from those interested in human health and the well-being of salmon stocks in the Teifi, clearly had some influence and eventually, in 1878, Whitehall sent an official into the area. This was one Walpole, Inspector of Salmon Fisheries, who was instrumental in establishing "codes of practice" whereby water flowing from lead mines had to be carried through catchpits before discharging into nearby streams and rivers. This measure, temporarily at least, quelled local anxieties[9].

Running hurriedly through Pontrhydfendigaid the Teifi is received by the 792 hectare nature reserve of Cors Caron, to which access is available to permit holders by way of a series of well laid-out paths, courtesy of the Nature Conservancy Council and West Wales Naturalist's Trust. Towards the end of the last major ice age a barrier of moraine was deposited above Tregaron across the whole width of the valley, a shallow lake forming behind it. Very gradually, almost imperceptibly, open water vegetation was succeeded by reeds, fen peat and sphagnum moss, leading eventually to the development of three great raised bogs, almost 30 feet above the level of the original lake. These bogs, and the areas adjacent to them, provide a rich habitat for plants, animals and birds. Frogs and lizards lurk in the brackish water while the streams running into the Teifi are host to the water shrew, otter, trout and eel. Among the willow and birch scrub on the edge of the bog, finches, flycatchers and tits look down upon the warblers, bunting and water-rail and upwards towards the buzzards, kites and sparrowhawks hunting over the fen. The whole is pervaded by the melancholy call of the curlew and the doom-laden croak of the carrion crow.

For centuries the bog provided local people with grazing for their livestock, rushes for bedding and peat for fuel. The labour-intensive task of peat collecting was particularly important to the local economy. The peat was cut in the early summer to a depth of almost six feet, stacked to dry, and then carried away in the autumn before rising water levels made passage with horse and cart impossible. Back in the 1920's a consortium of entrepreneurs conceived the idea of mechanising the job of peat cutting and subsequently selling the material for stable bedding. But this venture soon fizzled out as did an earlier idea for

Cors Caron

distilling bog peat with the object of commercially producing oil, paraffin and ammonia gas[10]. Somehow the ancient bog seems to have rejected these and similar projects (which, of course, threatened its continued existence), and only allowed small-scale peat cutting, a practice which continued until cheap alternative fuels became readily available in the 1950s.

Now a mature river, the Teifi leaves the nature reserve by way of Pont Einon, a sturdy and elegant bridge whose original may have been named after Einon Sais, abbot of Strata Florida in 1281. The earlier, and in all probability, wooden bridge would have resounded to the clatter of carts carrying from Aber-arth the freestone used to such marvellous effect for the decorative work of the Abbey. More than five centuries later, John Rees, parish clerk of Tregaron, supervised the building of a bridge of three finely-sprung arches to carry the old turnpike road across the river, and it is much to the credit of the local authorities that they have allowed this to remain despite subsequent road

Pont Einon, Tregaron

rationalisation[11]. A few hundred yards to the south west of Pont Einon stands the substantial farm of Penybont where a 17th century house built by the Herbert family was replaced in the mid 18th century by a further building erected under the direction of Thomas Johnes of Llanfair Clydogau and Dolaucothi, bucolic father of the sophisticated, urbane and far-famed Thomas Johnes of Hafod (SN 669612). For most of the time Penybont was occupied by agents of the Hafod estate, thereby serving as a useful place for members of the Johnes family to break the journey between Hafod and Dolaucothi. A financially-embarrassed Thomas Johnes junior eventually sold the property in 1805 to a local family called Rowlands whose resting places are marked by substantial tombstones on the north side of Tregaron churchyard[12].

Further on the Teifi skirts Tregaron, an unpretentious little town dominated by its church rising monumentally from an oval mound, traditionally accommodating the remains of Caron, the patron saint. As the last lowland station before the epic trip across the mountains to England, Tregaron was for centuries before 1900 an important centre for the cattle droving trade. Here mobs of cattle, sheep and horses were assembled and the bodies and souls of men fuelled in pub, church and chapel before they undertook the arduous and hazardous journey eastwards[13]. Often these rough and boisterous men would carry with them, either for their own use or for sale in England, samples of the socks and gloves produced by the women of Tregaron and the surrounding countryside. Indeed, the hosiery trade was about as important to Tregaron as cattle droving and many of those families occupying the little cottages to the south of the church spent their time carding and spinning wool—much of it gathered from hedgerows and ditch-bottoms—before knitting socks and gloves for sale. The spinning wheel and handloom were common objects in cottage and farmhouse alike, with women, children and the disabled all working to produce knitted and woven goods to supplement what was often a meagre family income. "Knitting evenings" were regular social diversions and the singing

21

and harp-playing which enlivened these occasions may have compensated knitters for the fact that the profit on a pair of stockings in 1810 rarely exceeded 3d.[14]. Drovers apart, the itinerant stocking dealer, plying his wares principally in the south Wales industrial districts, was the main outlet for cottage knitware. Like the drovers but unlike most of the denizens of Tregaron, this highly-respected and forthright visitor travelled far and wide and his arrival was eagerly awaited since it carried both the promise of hard cash and news of fabulous and remarkable events taking place in the world outside. The stocking dealer, commented someone over a century ago, "... belongs to the honest old-fashioned age himself, of coats that lasted years, not a season—of cloth that was made to wear, not merely to sell—an age when men spoke what they felt (and) cared nothing about what the world thought"[15].

If it was the centre of the world to its own residents, Tregaron was reckoned a poor sort of place by English travellers of the 18th and early 19th centuries, one dismissing it as having nothing, "... on which the eye can rest with tolerable satisfaction". Though the town was blessed with three shops and eleven inns, the latter were far from salubrious. Hucks observed, "Tregaron is a miserable hole, in which, however, we were constrained to sleep, and to break the windows in our bedrooms to let in the fresh air"[16]. Nor did the food commend itself to any but the strongest constitutions. J. T. Barber and his companion sat down to, "... a capacious dish of eggs and bacon for our dinner; but, though it was not more than ordinarily strong and greasy for the wilds of Wales, we grew delicate and, leaving our meal almost untasted, pursued our journey ..."[17].

In fairness to the memory of the old innkeepers of Tregaron, the English traveller has always been less than charitable in his remarks concerning both food and accommodation away from his native hearth! Things could not have been all that bad, for within this little whitewashed town of cottages, barns and stables there thrived a vibrant community. In 1839 residents included saddlers, glovers, weavers, tanners, bookbinders, brewers, hosiers, hatters, butchers and bootmakers along with a host of nonconformist divines. Early in the century, principally to help with the financing of the cattle trade, a branch of the Aberystwyth and Tregaron Bank was opened in the town, providing an important service for local tradesmen. Issuing its own notes of denominations ranging from 10/- to £20 and imprinted with fine impressions of black sheep, *Banc y Ddafad Ddu,* as it became known, enjoyed a brief hey-day before collapsing along with many other banks in the depressed years following the Napoleonic Wars. The fall of the bank must have had a traumatic local effect since its proprietors, John Evans, Joseph Jones and William Davies paid out a mere 6/8 in the pound after their bankruptcy in 1827.[18].

In the fat and prosperous years of the Napoleonic Wars, fair days and holidays were busy times for the bank as farmers rode in from the surrounding countryside and a multitude of dealers, drovers, peddlers and small tradesmen converged on the town. Equally busy was the town constable and his officers, obliged to deal with the drunkenness and petty crimes which usually went hand-in-hand with the razzmatazz of hiring and livestock fairs. Alive to the deterrent value to the petty felon of the "short, sharp shock", the parish council decided in 1814, to pay Thomas Davies, carpenter, the sum of 3 guineas for a new set of oak stocks. Customarily a pillory was erected close to the stocks but this does not seem to have been used in Tregaron. In nearby Lampeter, however, the pillory was very much in evidence as Thomas John found to his cost after he had been convicted of stealing a pair of shoes and buckles in 1754. The unhappy John was ordered to be stripped naked to the waist and whipped by the Master of the House of Correction, "... until his body be bloody"[19]. Such a punishment would certainly concentrate the mind! Presumably, though, the severity of the whipping would depend upon how sadistic the man with the whip and how popular (or otherwise) the individual occupying the pillory might be.

Maybe some of those who experienced the ignominy of the stocks or felt the lick of hide across their backs rest in Tregaron's charmingly unkempt churchyard. Here, amongst the dandelions, plantains and ragwort lie farmers, curriers, hosiers and innkeepers, all watched over by the stern figure of the renowned preacher William Rees Thomas who died towards the end of the last century. A son of Tregaron and student of Jesus College, Oxford, Thomas managed the twin feats of preaching in no less than 661 different churches, and siring eleven children of whom six followed him into the priesthood[20]. Almost two centuries before Thomas went to his reward there died, at the age of eighty six, one Daniel Rowland, whose gravestone grimly reminds us of our inevitable fate:

"Stay worldling stay, here mayst thou see
The frailty of thy life in mee
Then live to learn that dye thou must
And after come to judgement just".

Or, more simply and pathetically as with the tiny Elizabeth Johnes, laid low by some ailment in the spring of 1726:

"Sooner or later go we must
Into our den beneath the dust".

Like most country people in days gone by the stalwarts of Tregaron were prey to all manner of superstitions. The mayflower never came into the house, elaborate means were taken to avoid the evil eye and all manner of conscious and unconscious rituals enacted to propitiate gods and spirits much older than Christianity. Small wonder then that regular visits were made to the holy well of Ffynnon Caron near Glan-brennig to the south of the town. Holy wells are common throughout England and Wales, some noted for the quality of their water, others for some celebrated local custom, tradition or legend. Ffynnon Caron's special attributes apparently derived from supposed links with the shadowy Saint Caron, although it might equally have been a pagan site—with attendant supernatural powers—long before the saint established himself at Tregaron. Like Caron, the early monks and anchorites tended to settle at locations with source of fresh water nearby, and if this had previous sacred associations for a local pagan cult, so much the better for the new

In Tregaron Churchyard

evangelists who, in a sense, would be given a flying start! As time passed, the older associations faded and as the local saint's reputation increased, so the tales of the well's miraculous origins and powers became enshrined in folk memory. When Tregaron children drank sugared water at Ffynnon Caron on the Saturday before Easter were they re-enacting an aspect of the Good Friday scene? Or may it not have been some arcane pagan ritual of regeneration?

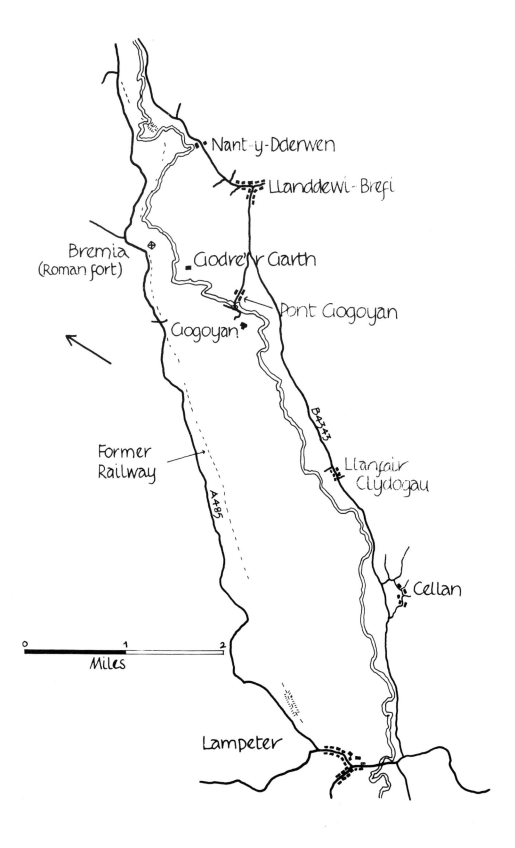

Nant-y-Dderwen

Llanddewi-Brefi

Bremia
(Roman fort)

Godre'r Garth

Pont Gogoyan

Gogoyan

Former
Railway

B4343

Llanfair
Clydogau

A485

Cellan

0   1   2

Miles

Lampeter

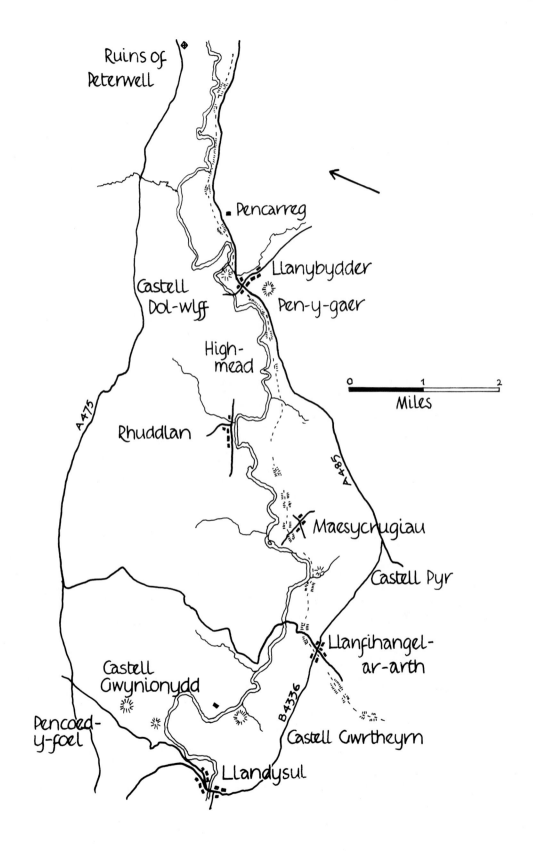

Ruins of Peterwell

Pencarreg

Castell Dol-wlff

Llanybydder

Pen-y-gaer

High-mead

A475

Rhuddlan

A485

Maesycrugiau

Castell Pyr

Llanfihangel-ar-arth

Castell Gwynionydd

Pencoed-y-foel

B4336

Castell Gwrtheyrn

Llandysul

0   1   2
Miles

CHAPTER TWO

Saints, Chieftains and Sinners:
Tregaron to Llandysul

Between Tregaron and Lampeter the River Teifi runs through low-lying meadowland. If one ignores the awful modern farm buildings, testament to the willingness of governments to encourage the expansion of agriculture regardless of aesthetic and environmental cost, this is delightful dairy country. Hedgebanks are crowned by light beech hedges containing fine specimens of oak, ash and maple, their sides festooned with stitchwort, violets, campions and bluebells. As a reminder, in a sense, of the rôle of hedgerow timber in times past, the occasional oak gate breaks the monotony of cheap tubular steel while the ubiquitous, (and now decaying) churnstands recall those relatively recent days when one could walk the lanes of Cardiganshire without risk of destruction by a 20 ton milk tanker! A man raised in the agrarian

deserts of Essex or the desecrated chalk downs of Wiltshire might be forgiven for thinking that here the farmer, that much-vaunted "custodian of the landscape", was still alive to his traditional duties towards the land. But any comforting thoughts along these lines soon evaporate when, as he wanders the river bank beyond Tregaron he stumbles upon a melancholy pile of rusty cars. The chassis of a Morris Minor, the rusting carcasses of redundant Fords and the brummagem fragments of a Datsun reside dodo-like alongside the burnt-out frame of a long forgotten Austin Somerset. This sort of rural vandalism can surely no longer be tolerated in a country whose economic base is now so decayed that it has to rely upon tourism for a major part of its national income.

The Teifi beyond Lampeter

The country skirting the river below Tregaron has been long-settled, and when the Romans built their fort of nearby *Bremia* much of the land thereabouts was under cultivation. Farms like Godre'r Garth (SN 644557), Nant-y-dderwen (SN 665568), and Gogoyan (SN 639542), all mentioned, for example, in the marriage settlement of Thomas Jones of Olmarch to his wife Elizabeth in 1699, had been established centuries previously and it is likely that these and other local farms, their nineteenth century houses adorned with extensions and patios, occupy settlement sites of considerable antiquity[21]. The river flows by these venerable holdings through meadows of buttercups, plantains, ladies smock and meadowsweet, interspersed with "improved" pastures, barren of virtually everything but ryegrass nourished with artificial fertilisers. It is a wonderful place to be in late May. Alders hang gracefully from the river bank, swifts swoop low over the water, wild duck are raucous among the reeds and cows stretch lazily in the flickering sunlight.

Above the fine bridge at Pont Gogoyan the Teifi is joined by a modest tributary, the Brefi, a mile or so from Llanddewibrefi (SN 641548). A typical Cardiganshire village with two pubs, a shop, a stout and rather grim church and a general air of calm and tranquillity, Llanddewibrefi stands with its back towards the empty mountains and its face square on to the lush meadows between the Teifi and the Aeron. This quiet, elegant little place was well-known to several of the more important scholars and religious figures of medieval Wales, and even to St. David himself. Christianity had been established and had become a regular feature of daily life well before David's time. Following the withdrawal of the Romans and the subsequent reversion to paganism of many of the peoples of the west, evangelising Irish monks sallied forth in wicker-framed and hide-covered boats in the hope of bringing salvation to their Celtic brethren[22].

Initially the early Irish evangelists followed the Eastern tradition of asceticism whereby isolation, fasting and constant vigil supposedly left the mind free for the contemplation of God. But, being mere mortals, few of them could tolerate sustained isolation and they eventually came to form monastic communities for the purposes of mutual support. Here they lived within a framework of strict discipline, sharing all in common, practising severe privations and passing their days in a soul-purifying combination of hard physical labour and the contemplation of eternity. Modern St. David's, a meeting place of important land and sea routes became a significant monastic centre of which,' according to Rhygyfarch's "Life of St. David" written around 1095, David became Archbishop by popular acclaim. Like so many of the Celtic saints, David was credited with all manner of legendary achievements, one of the more spectacular and famous being linked to his visit to Llanddewibrefi in the late sixth century for the purpose of expunging from the Church what was subsequently to become known as the Pelagian heresy. Pelagius, a Celt (and probably Irish), had visited Rome in the previous century where he had conceived a doctrine denying Divine Grace in favour of free-will to pursue God's purpose. For harbouring and attempting to foster such dangerous ideas the unfortunate man was condemned as a heretic in 418. Yet his views remained influential long after his death, much to the annoyance of the Church authorities who did everything in their power to purge the heresy. In the remote reaches of west Wales Pelagianism had become well-rooted and it was decided to hold a synod at Llanddewibrefi in the hope of turning people's hearts and minds away from this unpalatable doctrine. The synod, apparently, attracted crowds so great that no-one could make himself heard above the clamour and din. After much deliberation the assembled clerics agreed to send for David on the grounds that he was the only man around who could, at one and the same time, speak loudly and clearly and be convincing in his arguments. The saint, it seems, was none too keen and could only be prevailed upon after "repeated applications and earnest entreaty". But at last he arrived and having rejected the pile of clothes which had been hurriedly thrown together to form a speaking platform, he addressed the crowd from level ground. And then, wonder of wonders, the earth rose beneath his feet and a white dove settled on his shoulder! Hence the origin-myth of the mound now occupied by the church[23].

In 1693 the great antiquary Edward Lhuyd visited Llanddewibrefi church and noted an inscribed stone above the chancel door. On a return visit several years later he had the stone removed and after some trouble managed to decipher the early 7th century script: "Hic jacet Idnert, filius Jacobi qui occisus fuit propter predam santi david" (Here lies Idnert, son of Jacob who was killed on account of the plunder (robbery) of David's sanctuary). Only part of the stone can be seen today, much of it having been broken up in the 19th century and incorporated face-inwards into the west wall of the nave. Thus we only have Lhuyd's, and later Sir Richard Colt Hoare's word for it, but this seems on the face of it to have been the earliest written reference to Wales's patron saint. The church, incidentally, boasts other ancient stones with both Latin and Ogham inscriptions, together with a modern statue of David attired in the simple clothes of a "tribal bishop"[24]. The early stones managed to survive the 1781 restoration (towards which the Duke of Gloucester contributed £40) and a later restoration in 1873 when the church was re-roofed and refitted under the architectural direction of R. J. Withers and the financial management of the vicar, Lewis Rowland, who raised most of the necessary cash by public appeal[25].

In the wake of his "conquest" of Wales in 1282-3, Edward I needed all the friends he could get and was therefore keen to appoint to positions of authority men who would be able to enforce the royal will in the newly-conquered territories. Hence the appointment of Thomas Bek, sometime keeper of the King's Wardrobe, to the bishopric of St. David's, a post which he held until his death in 1293. Like other English clerics of the time, and in accordance with royal policy, Bek was determined to bring the Celtic churches in his diocese more securely under Latin rule and thus to ensure uniformity of both liturgical practice and monastic organisation. He disapproved particularly of the brotherhoods of married Celtic clergy whose monastic gatherings formulated their own rules and rejected the authority of the specific "rules" laid down for Latin monasteries. Having founded a collegiate church at Llangadog in Carmarthenshire in 1283, he extended the process of "latinisation" to Llanddewibrefi four years later by ordering the disbandment of the local clergy and their replacement by a college of secular canons charged with daily performance of the Latin service. By way of this much-resented action, he was enabled to add to the limited prebends of his cathedral at St. David's a number of new prebends with which he could reward deserving (English?) clerics. The college was dissolved by Edward VI in 1549[26].

In the library of Jesus College, Oxford, lies a manuscript volume containing one of the the the fullest and most important collections of philosophical tracts in the Welsh language. Compiled in 1346, probably by one of the canons in Bek's foundation at Llanddewibrefi, "The Book of the Anchorite" was produced anonymously under the patronage of Gruffudd ap Llywelyn, scion of a local princely family to the forefront in the patronage of Welsh letters. Typically, the author remained anonymous, fearful of the sin of pride or of inducing the sin of envy in his readers. "I have made no mention of my own name", he wrote, "lest these works should be marred by envy. But rather let the reader pray that the name of him who wrote them should be written in Heaven and never blotted out from the book of life"[27].

As the hair-shirted anchorite sat in his drafty cell laboriously penning his lofty thoughts, the local peasantry tilled their lands and tended their cattle. Some, too, worked the local lead-mines of which, according to the Black Book of St. David's, an early 14th century survey of the bishop's lands and rents, "the profits were rare"[28]. Less so, however, the profits of the silver mine on the banks of the Teifi at Llanfair Clydogau some three miles distant from Llanddewibrefi. The discovery in 1760 of a vein of silver ore among the lead deposits close to the point where the busy Clywedog River joins the Teifi is generally credited to one Chauncy Townsend, M.P., alderman of the City of London and mining entrepreneur. Described by a rival as a "mean, designing, ignorant fellow",

The bridge at Llanfair Clydogau

Townsend successfully worked the vein for a number of years, reputedly recovering up to 87 ounces of silver per ton of lead. By the early 1800's the mine was in the hands of the canny, if rather disreputable, Job Sheldon, a prominent figure in the public life of Aberystwyth whose later days were overshadowed by charges of corruption. After Sheldon had surrendered his lease several speculators tried their hands, the last being the able mining engineer John Taylor who, though still able to recover 80 ounces of silver for each ton of mined lead, gave up in the 1840's and the mine seems subsequently to have been abandoned[29]. The old shafts are now filled with domestic rubbish, the stonework originally supporting the great water wheel having been removed in 1933 and used in the building of the present church hall—at a cost of £370 as I am informed by its builder, Mr. Gwyn Evans. But not all has disappeared, for several of the cottages and houses around the site have been converted to their present use from the mining offices, drying rooms and smithy. "Swyddfa Fawr", for instance, was originally the main administrative office. This is now a charming house surrounded by a fine garden. In creating this garden the present occupier has unearthed the stone foundations of a substantial structure which may be all that remains of the manor house of the Johnes family of Llanfair, Hafod, and Dolaucothi.

Meandering quietly through the meadows south of Lampeter the Teifi skirts the boundaries of the Peterwell estate, from the mid 17th century the home of the Evans and Lloyd families. The squires of Peterwell had never enjoyed the most convivial relations with the local people and the succession of the appalling Sir Herbert Lloyd to the life-tenancy of the estate in 1755 gave cause for concern. This tempestuous and mendacious scoundrel terrorised the countryside and aided by his ruthless henchmen restored to almost unbelievable skulduggery and violence to further his social and political ambitions. Such were the dramatic events associated with Lloyd's fourteen-year

Peterwell

Lampeter and Llanybydder the Teifi runs through level, tightly-grazed meadows and in doing so it occasionally edges towards the high embankment of the old railway line, now a happy profusion of ash, sycamore and willow and a bewildering variety of wild flowers. In a national landscape increasingly subject to the rapine of modern agricultural practice and progressively devastated by agro-chemicals, such sites may prove to be among the few remaining havens for wildlife by the middle of the next century.

Abandoned railway bridge, beyond Lampeter

occupation of Peterwell that he became something of a local bogey-man after his death and it is widely believed that his restless ghost lurks about the ruins of the Peterwell mansion, a few hundred yards from the river[30] (SN 570478). And how forlorn these ruins are! Gone the four great towers, topped with their golden crowns; gone the splendid roof gardens where fountains played among the shrubs and flowers; and gone the terraces, parterres and canals. Today a shadowy avenue of trees leading off the Lampeter road carries the visitor to two pitiful stumps of towers and a jumbled pile of masonry intermixed with bits of redundant farm machinery. Great ash trees erupt from the bowels of the mansion casting a gloomy and almost malignant shadow over the surrounding fields; nettles and brambles infest the crumbling stone and from somewhere nearby the stench of a sheep's carcase drifts on the wind. So much for Peterwell.

For the best part of its journey between

A visit to Pencarreg Church, standing on higher ground to the south of the river, is a worthwhile diversion if for nothing more than the charm of the churchyard with its early gravestones and spectacular views of the pastoral landscape of the Teifi (SN 535450). In a tomb close to the church and surrounded by impressive iron railings rest the remains of the celebrated poet Daniel Evans (Daniel Ddu o Geredigion), known widely as "the Cardigan-

The tomb of Daniel Ddu o Geredigion: Pencarreg Churchyard

shire Burns". Born in 1792 at Maesymynach near Lampeter, Evans became a fellow of Jesus College, Oxford and after a period as chaplain at the Royal Military Asylum in Northampton he returned to Wales in the late 1820's where he abandoned the clerical life and became a recluse. His collected works were published in 1831 under the title *Gwinllan y Bardd,* thirteen years before his death on 28th March 1846[31]. According to that splendid craftsman, lecturer, stargazer and cave explorer, Thomas Jenkins of Llandeilo, Evans, a chronic depressive "committed suicide by suspending himself by his handkerchief"[32]. As a general rule suicides were not interred in the local churchyard, or not at least in the consecrated parts of that churchyard, unless the incumbent of the parish considered them to be deserving cases. Evans was clearly deserving of the privilege since the Bishop's Transcripts testify to his burial and in so doing indicate the affection and respect which he enjoyed among the community[33]

The Teifi is carried beyond Pencarreg by a series of meanders to the outskirts of Llanybydder, a quiet little town periodically enlivened by its cattle market and colourful horse fairs. Above the bridge carrying the road from Llanwnnen into the town, the river has cut a steep escarpment on its right bank. Here, on this readily defensible site, some Iron Age chieftain threw up a castle of the incomplete ringwork type which, until recently, remained in a well-preserved condition thanks to the enthusiasm of a local landowner. The Ordnance Survey 1 inch map stoutly proclaims the continued existence of "Castell Dol-Wlff" but in fact it has all but disappeared; its banks have been piled up with rubbish and its ditch filled with junk to make way for, of all things, a caravan (SN 520445). The degradation of this interesting Iron Age location has taken place *despite* representations having been made to official bodies respecting the decline of the site. Peering through the trees around "Castell Dol-Wlff" towards the hill above Llanybydder and to the south of the Teifi, it is possible to make out the form of the large hillfort of Pen-y-gaer (SN 524434). Whether the two sites were tribally or strategically associated is not altogether clear. In any event, if either was occupied when the Romans drove the main branch of their great road "Sarn Helen" along the bottom of the hill crowned by Pen-y-gaer, the pulses of the surveyors may have raced a little more quickly than usual[34].

Embraced partially by a great curve in the river between Llanybydder and the hamlet of Rhuddlan is the demesne of the Highmead Estate (SN 502432). Originally the property of the Evans family who spawned magistrates and sheriffs in profusion in the 18th and 19th centuries, the estate has long since been broken-up, the mansion having been converted into a residential school under the control of the local authority. Built originally in the late 1770's, this replaced an older house laying closer to the river. Having suffered the dual indignities of unharmonious 19th century accretions and occupation by American troops during World War II, the house was "renovated" by Dyfed County Council who, in an act of extraordinary architectural vandalism, removed the fine (if decrepit) stone balustrade from the front of the building and replaced it with plain galvanised steelwork.

Among the properties included in the Highmead Estate were the collection of riverside houses and farms known as Rhuddlan Teifi. This tiny hamlet's principal claim to fame reposes in the fact that it is mentioned in that masterpiece of European medieval literature *The Mabinogion,* a collection of romances and tales with their roots in the dawn of the Celtic world which came to be written down in *The White Book of Rhydderch* (1300—1325) and *The Red Book of Hergest* (1375—1425)[35]. According to one of the tales, the hero Pryderi, son of Pwyll, had his court or *llys* on a spot close to the riverside in the magnificently-wooded Highmead Park[36]. Pure romance perhaps; but the nature of the site, defended by a deep river and surrounded by fertile land, would have made it an ideal spot for a chieftain to settle in tranquil times. Surrounded by his own bond-men, servants and friends, this would be a fine place for Pryderi—or someone like him—to take his leisure. Hunting by day, drinking by night, giving and receiving presents, graciously accepting tribute and listen-

Highmead: late 19th century

33

ing to the fulsome praises of the bards would have been the enviable lot of the resident of the *llys* at Rhuddlan Teifi.

Mentioned by Giraldus Cambrensis as a grange "... situate in fertile and arable land, fully cultivated by numerous ploughs and fertilised by innumerable sheep and cattle in ample pastures", Rhuddlan Teifi was eventually granted by the Lord Rhys to the Abbey of Whitland. The grange remained under the control of the abbey for almost four centuries and according to the *Valor Ecclesiasticus* (1535), drawn up around the time of the Dissolution, its full extent encompassed the area occupied by six farms separate units in the early part of the present century. These were Cefn Rhuddlan Issa, Cefn Rhuddlan Ganol, Cefn Rhuddlan Uchaf, Dolau Bach, Dolau Canol and Dolau Uchaf[37].

Below Rhuddlan the river negotiates a rocky gorge at Maesycrugiau, a totally magical place where rapids above the bridge carrying the narrow road give way to quietly-flowing water through broad meadows and tree-lined banks. In the early phases of World War II some strategian or military planner built a pill-box on the bridge over the Teifi. Perhaps the man who ordered the construction of this surreal object had the idea of manning it himself; of risking the remote possibility of enemy fire in return for the sheer pleasure of contemplating the magnificence of the river and the quiet splendour of its banks! Whatever, the pill-box has now been happily converted into a wash-house by the family whose home adjoins it. Above the bridge, perched splendidly atop a great rock overlooking the gorge is the finely-restored 13th century parish church of Llanllwni. Standing proudly in its ample churchyard beside a medieval motte, this church must surely occupy one of the most impressive ecclesiastical sites in this part of Wales.

Llanllwni Church

Maesycrugiau

High above the south bank, a mile beyond Maesycrugiau and on a plateau occupying the angle between the stream of Nant Cwmdu and the Teifi is a large earthwork known as Castell Pŷr (SN 469400). Extensive views of the surrounding countryside, a 20 foot high outer bank and a 10 foot wide inner ditch bespeak a defensive function for this bracken-covered structure, although by whom it was built and against whom

Teifiside from Castell Pŷr

it was defended is an open question. Perhaps the site was in some way associated with Castell Gwrtheyrn, a large hillfort currently lying in thick woodland a mile or more down-river (SN 433402). Although the embankments and ditches of Castell Gwrtheyrn are now largely demolished or infilled it is still just possible to make out what was clearly a well-defended entrance to the south-west. Local tradition has it that this hillfort was one of the strongholds of the notorious Vortigern (Gwrtheyrn), a Romanised Briton who seized the opportunity to dismantle a good deal of Britain during the chaos following the departure of the Imperial troops. Whether this riparian fortress was Vortigern's "headquarters", or whether Gwrtheyrnion near Builth Wells should be so described we are never likely to establish with certainty. We do know, however, that Vortigern was acknowledged as founder of the ruling dynasty of the kindgom of Powys and that like other Romano-British chieftains he made the fatal mistake of hiring Saxon mercenaries to help counter Pictish invasion attempts. The floodgates soon opened. Wave upon wave of these vigorous and blood-thirsty pirates surged up the river valleys driving all before them, taking advantage of political and military conflict among the native Britons to press deeper and deeper into the heartland. A peace conference was eventually held resulting in that unspeakable massacre enshrined in Welsh annals as *Brad y Cyllyll Hirion*, ("The Treason of the Long Knives"). Thus was sown the seed of mutual distrust between Celt and Saxon which was to germinate and flourish over many centuries.

However battle-scarred and world-weary the chieftain holding sway at Castell Gwrtheyrn may have been, his spirits must have soared as he looked down towards the cultivated riverside fields where his bondmen harvested ripe corn as it struggled through a blaze of poppy and columbine. The river still flows through the same fields, now supporting species-rich grasslands where butterflies and dragonflies dance in the sun. Downriver from the bridge at Llanfihangel-ar-arth and on the opposite bank to Castell Gwrtheyrn, Jersey cows graze the meadows of Llanfair (SN 433409). This fine old house with its Georgian front and almost com-

The Bridge at Llanfihangel-ar-Arth

Llanfair

pletely unspoilt set of early 19th century farm buildings sits comfortably at the edge of the mature woods wrapping themselves around the hillside above the river. Thinking men in Georgian Britain talked much of the means whereby architecture and landscaping would "improve" nature. Wittingly or otherwise, the man who conceived the present Llanfair did precisely that, and in the scenically-rich middle reaches of the Teifi valley there are few places where "art" and "nature" coexist in so harmonious a manner.

The Dark Age rulers of Ceredigion claimed descent from Cunedda, a Brythonic Celtic chieftain occupying land around the Firth of Forth in late Roman times. Although Cunedda and his fabulous sons now appear to be imaginary fabrications of the bards of the court of the 9th century king, Maelgwyn Gwynedd, there certainly seems to have been a connection between Ceredigion and North Briton in the sub-Roman period. Legend has it that Cunedda and his sons were invited to Gwynedd and subsequently to Ceredigion to help stem the flow of Goidelic-speaking Irish immigrants who appeared in ever-increasing numbers in the late 4th and early 5th centuries[38]. Whoever these northern warriors were—if they existed at all—they largely failed to put a stop to the Irish incursions so that throughout the 5th century dense settlements of these turbulent invaders were established throughout much of southern Dyfed to the extent that most of the area south of the Teifi became predominantly Goidelic in speech. Irish settlement continued well into the 6th century and (presumably) as the level of violence declined, locals came to accept the presence of the immigrants with their strange language and Ogham script[39]. Intermarriage would soon have become common so that in time cultural origins would have become progressively blurred.

While they were bravely struggling to hold existing Irish elements in check and to prevent the incursion of others, local tribesmen in the mid-Teifi valley area established a base at Castell Gwynionydd (SN 424421). This ringwork enclosure, occupying a high position above what is now the minor road linking Llandysul with Capel Dewi, enjoyed panoramic views of the countryside on both banks of the river. Bounded on three sides by massive embankments almost 20 feet high with an impressive 10 foot wide outer ditch, the eastern side of the enclosure required no defensive earthworks, relying for security upon the very steep slope rising from the meadows alongside the Teifi. The entrance is clearly visible to the north-west while to the east the embankment increases in height, possibly to accommodate a lookout tower. Hard by the bracken-shrouded and tree-grown embankment of Castell Gwynionydd there stands, in the corner of the field to the south-east, an irregularly-shaped stone some 4 feet high. Marked on the earlier Ordnance Survey maps as a "standing stone" it is tempting to associate this massive stone with some arcane ritual carried out at Castell Gwynionydd or the nearby hillfort site of Pencoed-y-foel (SN 425427). Equally, of course, like so many standing stones, this one could have been dumped conveniently in the present spot by some Georgian or Victorian farmer keen to get rid of an obstruction to his plough.

High above Castell Gwynionydd and beyond the lovely sessile oak woodlands of Coedfoel is a univallate hillfort occupying some 4 acres. Pencoed-y-foel, as the site is known, was surrounded by a simple ditch and bank which, although much-degraded, is still readily apparent to the south side. A substantial spread of large surface stones in adjacent grazing land may represent the remains of that part of the embankment not used for making the 18th and 19th century enclosure walls cutting through the fort.

I have drawn attention to several hillforts either visible from Teifiside or within a brief walk from the river banks. Considering the voluminous literature on the subject it is perhaps surprising that no-one can identify with absolute certainty the specific function of these often enigmatic structures although excavations currently under way at Cellan may extend our understanding[41]. Of the 1500 or so hillforts in Britain, mainly built between 1000 and 500 B.C., some may have been tribal capitals, houses of powerful local chieftains, or temporary refuges in times of trouble, while others were permanent settlements for whole communities and their livestock. Since excavation has rarely revealed high quality artefacts and precious metals, but rather the day-to-day functional goods of a working population, one might suggest—and this is mere speculation—that the latter generally occupied the hillfort, perhaps even maintaining it as a bolthole for a chieftain and his retainers in time of war. In the deteriorating climatic conditions of the early Iron Age there would have been a desperate struggle between communities for diminishing areas of farmland and leaders of those communities would have sought to maintain a well defended sanctuary both for themselves and their dependent peasants. In any event the hillfort was a special construction, the "capital" of the surrounding area and a symbol of the power of a local magnate. Individual hillforts went through successive phases of abandonment, reoccupation and reconstruction over a long period and if most were largely redundant by Norman times, others proved valuable defensive sites for medieval Welsh princes as they struggled for power one against the other or

together against the organised might of the Norman invaders.

In the past religion and ritual were essential elements in social cohesion. "Primitive" though the earlier occupants of the hillforts around the Teifi may have been, they required contact with the world beyond the battlefield and ploughland; the world of the spirit, beyond death itself. The psychological need of the individual for a link with the spiritual world was paralleled in the community's requirement for ensuring fruitful harvests and success in battle. Group veneration of a particular deity would help with the latter, at the same time bringing people together in a sense of common purpose. We know very little of Celtic religious practice, yet there must have been an enormous variety of local pagan cults about which developed a complex of rituals perhaps involving human sacrifice and other forms of blood-letting. Recent studies of a coarse-grained sandstone head of typical "Celtic" type, originally found on farmland near Llandysul in the 1930's, suggest that in Roman-British times this area was the focal point of a particularly dark and sinister ritual involving a

The Teifi near Llandysul

38

Teifiside towards Llandysul

cult of the severed head. To the Celts the head was the repository of the soul and was accordingly an object of great veneration. Roman writers recall that besides regularly exhibiting the heads of slain enemies as symbols of their martial prowess, Celtic warriors enthusiastically partook of ritual headhunting. The Llandysul head, with its hollow eyes and swollen lips, bears close similarity both to Celtic bronzes and "severed heads" found elsewhere in Britain and may originally have been the centrepiece of some family shrine devoted to the propitiation of whatever god or demon protected the practitioners of the cult[42].

Standing monumentally on the banks of the Teifi in Llandysul itself is the church, a symbol of a far more durable faith. The church descends from the simple wattle-and-daub foundation of Tyssul (562-544 AD), son of Ceredig and cousin to St. David himself. Subsequently a wooden structure was built, being replaced in the 13th century by a stone church which incidentally, became one of the foundations whose emoluments helped to finance Bishop Bek's enterprise at Llanddewibrefi. Like most of the churches on

Teifiside the present building bears very little similarity to the original; a belfry loft and attendant bells were installed in the mid 18th century, the thatched roof was replaced with slates over a three year period up to 1783 and the whole was extensively "restored" in Victorian times[43]. Because the church needed to minister to such a wide area—over 17,500 acres—the medieval ecclesiastical authorities established six simply constructed "chapels of ease" at various localities in the parish. These fell out of use in the 19th century and subsequently succumbed to decay and dilapidation so that all trace of them has now disappeared. The decline of the chapels of ease and the concomitant rise of Nonconformity alarmed the Established Church and it was reported in the Religious Census of 1851 that a "cottage lecture" was delivered on alternate Sundays in a distant part of the parish in the (forlorn) hope that this would turn people away from the embrace of one of the ten local nonconformist chapels[44].

The present church has a rather dull and gloomy feel about it, due in part to the enthusiasm of the Victorian restorers who tore down

39

In Llandysul

the internal plaster and repointed the stonework with black cement. Besides several fine monuments to the Lloyd family of Alltyrodyn and Gilfachwen it houses little of interest, although exception must be made in the case of two antiquities. The first of these, the "Velvor" stone, originally languished in the stile leading into the churchyard but is now set in the north wall of the choir vestry and partially obscured by a cupboard. Inscribed in debased Roman capitals "Velvor filia Broho", the stone is one of the three Oghams in Ceredigion and in commemorating the life of Velvoria, the daughter of Brohomaglus, it becomes of immediate interest since very few early monumental inscriptions refer to women. The second antiquity, an ancient stone embellished with early Christian inscriptions, is incorporated into a modern stone altar in the Lady Chapel. Originally found in the fields between Castell Gwynionydd and Coedfoel, the stone has been somewhat fancifully described as an "altar" which might, at an earlier date, have been located at the site of Tyssul's first *llan*[45]. There is no evidence to support this dubious assertion.

As the Teifi curves gently away from the church and turns back on itself before flowing out of Llandysul, it passes under the bridge now carrying the busy A486 road to Carmarthen. Described by the antiquary Malkin around 1800 as a "venerable bridge", the present structure dates from the 1850's, having been built under the sponsorship of John Lloyd Davies of Alltyrodyn, M.P. and scourge of the Rebecca rioters, who currently lies with others of his family in the church of Bangor Teifi. The burden of maintaining the earlier bridge, like the others in the locality, fell upon the parish, and vestry meetings were often dominated by heated debate as to how this could be carried out at a minimum cost. In 1764 two men were engaged on a 21 year contract to look after the walls of the bridge. Being paid a mere 5 shillings per year, besides having to provide building materials themselves, they could hardly have been expected to approach the job with much enthusiasm and when the structure was seriously damaged by the river in 1782 they were summarily fired. The contract was then offered to Evan Rees, a local mason and publican. Clearly a canny individual, Rees would only agree to look after the bridge on condition that all vestry meetings were held in his pub *and* that his brother be granted the monopoly of making paupers' coffins for the village![47]

In and around Llandysul are numerous examples of excellent wrought ironwork, testaments to the skill of 19th century craftsmen in this *genre*. The splendid intricate gates at Llanfair, the gates of the church at Llandysul itself and grave enclosures in many local churchyards bespeak a thriving community of ironworkers and a middle-class clientèle prosperous enough to exploit their talents.

Contemporary Llandysul retains the architecture and some of the atmosphere of a Victorian country town. Horses may have been replaced by Landrovers; the smiths, coopers and chandlers may have given way to the agricultural merchant, yet most of Llandysul's visitors are farming folk, who come to buy provisions or execute business before returning to the farm in the valley. A century ago the town would have been quiet, unhurried, even somnolent. Today the pace has quickened and the visitor from the

Iron gates: Llanfair

Iron gates: Llandysul Churchyard

41

country does his shopping to the counterpoint of sounds totally alien to his Victorian ancestor. Lorries roar terribly through the main street; cement mixers chug lugubriously in the backyards of property "restorers" whose radio sets almost drown out the hum of the presses of the celebrated publishing house of Gwasg Gomer. Yet the Porth Hotel (if much-modernised) still caters for fishermen as it did a hundred years ago and the track running beside it towards the ancient ford across the Teifi can still be seen.

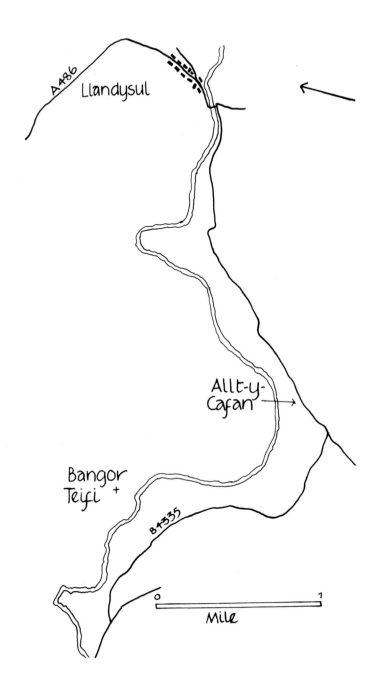

A486

Llandysul

Allt-y-
Cafan →

Bangor
Teifi +

B4335

0 ————————— 1
Mile

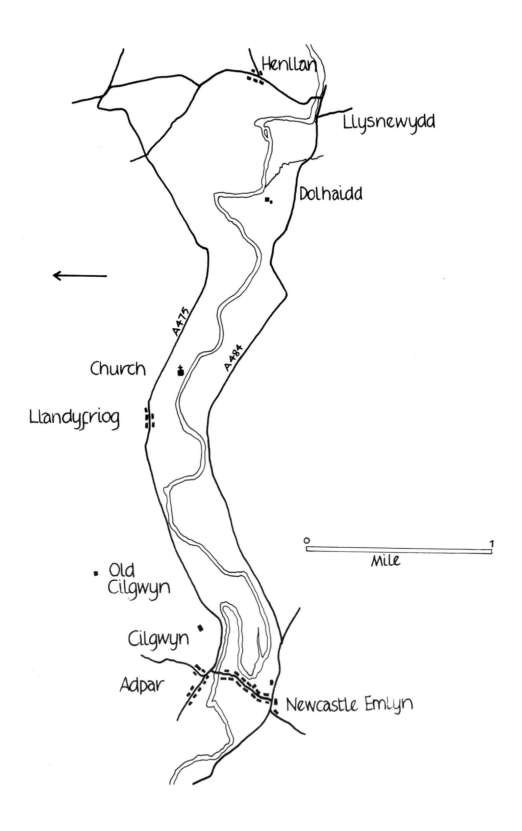

Henllan

Llysnewydd

Dolhaidd

A475

A484

Church

Llandyfriog

Old
Cilgwyn

Cilgwyn

Adpar

Newcastle Emlyn

0   1
Mile

CHAPTER THREE

Wool, Tories and Warfare;
Llandysul to Newcastle Emlyn

At Alltycafan, near Pentrecwrt, the Teifi enters a deep tree-hung gorge before flowing under the great bridge of Pont Allt-y-cafan (SN 387392). Another project sponsored by John Lloyd Davies, Pont Allt-y-cafan was built between 1839 and 1841, half the money required coming from Davies himself and the remainder from local subscription. A plaque on the parapet records that Davies's involvement (to the extent of £800) with the bridge, arose from a "conviction of its benefit to the country". He was originally to have provided a further £100 for "embellishments" to the basic structure, but was so incensed by the activities of the Rebecca rioters and by local insinuations that the bridge was being built to ease communications between his own two principal residences that he refused further assistance[49]. On the

Cardiganshire side of the river at Pont Allt-y-cafan, the bridge is overlooked by a distinctly sinister-looking pill-box from which, on the opposite bank, can be seen the recently-deserted remains of the Allt-y-cafan woollen mill. This rather melancholy sight should remind us that by the second half of the 19th century, the mid-Teifi valley had become the focal point for the Welsh woollen industry. As a part-time occupation, textile working had been widespread in the cottages and farmhouses of Dyfed since medieval times. The woven cloth was subsequently "fulled" in order to clean the fabric and consolidate its texture and as water-powered fulling mills, activating hammers to beat the cloth on a wooden frame, came into being in late medieval times, this aspect of the cloth trade became a capital-intensive operation beyond the

Alltycafan Mill

pocket of most cottagers. Early fulling mills (*pandy/pandai*) are recorded at St. Dogmaels (1291), Cilgerran (1326) and Rhuddlan Deifi (1539), while one was in operation at Pentre-cwrt in 1574. The domestic weaving industry had started to decline by the turn of the 19th century with the development of a primitive but effective "factory" system run mainly by farmer-weavers with the wherewithal to buy the relatively expensive handlooms. These were set up in long sheds and operated by farm labourers, often selected by their employers as much for their skills in weaving as for their abilities as husbandmen. With the growth of the industry's prosperity, aided by the invention of carding engines and other mechanical contrivances, the domestic handloom weaver became a rarity and most gave in to the inevitable and sought employment in the burgeoning factories. The Teifi valley was an ideal location for these developments. Water power was available from the river and its tributaries, the surrounding hills provided a ready source of wool and a market for flannel products was growing in the rapidly-expanding mining community of the South Wales valleys. By 1898 there were no less than nineteen specialist weaving factories in the parishes of Llangeler and Pen-boyr alone; new houses were built, villages and their inhabitants prospered and the religious, cultural and social life of the community bloomed[50]. The period between 1880 and the end of the Great War was one of tremendous growth in trade, nurtured by the almost insatiable demand for army uniforms of which untold numbers were to rot in the appalling mud of Flanders. But the inevitable slump followed the end of the war. Enormous quantities of Government-surplus stock flooded the market, thereby forcing down flannel prices, while the traditional local market in the mining valleys received a severe blow when the miners downed tools in the 1920s. To make matters worse, fashions were changing, with people beginning to favour knitwear at the expense of flannel and although quality flannel was still in demand, this was now being produced extensively in west Yorkshire by manufacturers who had invested wartime profits in re-tooling their factories with modern equipment capable

of producing the quality product required by the market. Like many British manufacturers of recent years, the mill-owners of the Teifi valley failed signally in this respect, preferring to make use of out-dated and second-hand machinery which in turn reduced their capacity to compete in the market place. This lack of initiative, just at the time when hard-headed enterpreneurship was really needed, may be connected with the fact that many of these Teifi factory owners were also part-time farmers, imbued with the "conservative" attitudes characterising the farming community until more recent years[51].

Allt-y-cafan was built in 1895 at the peak of the boom. It continued to produce woollen goods into the 1970's but gradually the range of products was reduced, workers were laid off and the factory eventually closed in 1981. It remains today as a decaying testament to Victorian energy and entrepreneurship. Windows are broken, slates are missing and grass grows in the gutters, directing rain on to the slow-rotting floors. Behind the boarded windows the smell of oil and the earthy tang of wool are still detectable against the background odour of decay. The mill shop is closed; the gaily-coloured tiles around the door are flaking away and the awnings over the windows are in tatters and ruins. What one wonders, will be the ultimate fate of this particular relic of our industrial past?

Between Allt-y-cafan and the little Victorian church of Bangor Teifi, standing high above the Cardiganshire bank, woodlands sweep down to the Teifi before giving way to open fields carrying the river in a series of successive meanders towards Henllan. Before it reaches Edward Ellis's fine bridge at Henllan, completed in the cataclysmic year of 1789, the river runs dramatically through a deep gorge of scarred rocks lined with unkempt woods of beech, ash and oak. Today's waterflow can be rather impressive, especially after a prolonged period of wet weather. In the remote past, when water from the melting ice-sheets covering much of the area west of Pumlumon surged into the Teifi valley, the rate of flow through this and the other gorges down river would have been awesome indeed. Glacial geologists have estimated that some 2000 square miles of melted ice drained

The Teifi near Henllan

into the Teifi valley, so that something in the order of 60,000 cubic feet per second of water thundered towards the sea, gouging and tearing its way through shale and rock in a stupendous torrent of enormous erosive power[52].

The Henllan gorge is "picturesque" in the strict sense of the term. The juxtaposition of rapids, woodlands (reputedly planted in the 18th century by the Lewes family of Llysnewydd) and a small Iron Age promontory fort (now almost impossible to make out) would have held a strong appeal for the late 18th century traveller. So too would Henllan Church, a few yards below the bridge, at that time partially ruinous, "romantically" encrusted with ivy and haunted by bats and barn owls (SN 354402). It is a terrible indictment of the present age that Henllan, like other churches along the Teifi, has to remain locked. What hope for the future when even ecclesiastical buildings have to be protected from the cancer of vandalism?

In a sense, the disappearance of the nearby mansion of Llysnewydd also reflects the uncaring times in which we live (SN 354398). In 1794 Colonel John Lewes decided to build himself a new house on a site occupied by his family since the mid 17th century, and had the happy idea of calling in the young John Nash as his architect. Nash had escaped from his early failures in London and having built Carmarthen Gaol and several other structures in the area was rapidly establishing a reputation which was to be muchenhanced upon the completion of Llysnewydd, a house of great charm and character[53]. The delicate and airy interior was later massacred and the external work shrouded in Victorian ironmongery, yet Nash's Llysnewydd remained a house of great architectural importance until the ravages of dry-rot struck in the 1960's. Colonel Lewes's ancestor reacted swiftly; dynamite was ordered and the mansion was blown to smithereens in 1971. In the summer of 1985 the skeleton of a tennis court and a forlorn looking gazebo were all that remained of Llysnewydd. A single mare galloped in the oakstudded parkland and rabbits scampered around

47

Llysnewydd: late 19th century

the decrepit stables and formerly elegant buildings of the home farm.

Cardiganshire is replete with the tattered remains of mansions and the tree-grown remnants of abandoned gentry houses, victims to the caprice of irresponsible owners, the profligate spending of patrimony or the terrible mortgage commitments which encumbered so many county families towards the end of the last century. Some, like Trawsgoed, Gogerddan and Highmead have survived as institutions of one sort or another and others have become farmhouses or residences of the newly rich. But many, if not most, have been allowed to fester and decay. A pile of rubble, seasonally dignified by the presence of the Caravan Club, is the only testament to the glories of Hafod; Llanina is a wind-blown carcase looking sadly out across Cardigan Bay and Bronwydd, that extraordinary Gothic phantasmagoria, is a mere shell. Ichabod! [54]

In old parkland on the Carmarthenshire side of the river, to the outskirts of Henllan, stands Dol-haidd, one fine old house that has survived the ravages of time (SN 346405). Dol-haidd is deserving of attention as the one-time home of David Lewis, a member of the "Society of Sea Sergeants", an organisation of obscure origins flourishing between the 1720's and 1760's. Although they vigorously denied ulterior political motives and claimed to spend their time in "processions, feasts, balls, and water-parties", membership of the Sea Sergeants was limited to High Tory gentlemen of south and west Wales and in 1722 several were listed as probable supporters of a Jacobite rising. Since they last met in 1763, after the accession of George III (and thus the collapse of Stuart hopes) they might previously have nourished Jacobite sympathies and seditious intentions. Equally they could have been little more than dyed-in-the-wool Tories who enjoyed the *frisson* of allegiance to a dangerous cause where there was little chance of one's supposed loyalties being put to the test. It was no doubt great fun, anyhow, to don one's Jacobite badge, to swill wine from one Jacobite glass and, as the wine took effect, to burst into good old Jacobite songs of the king beyond the sea and the little gentleman in velvet! [55]

Like other gentlemen of their class and time, the Sea Sergeants viewed the duel as the ultimate means of settling an affair of honour and this

48

patently absurd practice continued to be commonplace until well into Victorian times. The history and literature of the British abounds with examples of men (who should have known better) prepared to blast away with pistols or pierce each other with swords after a moment's provocation. A little way beyond Dol-haidd, close by where the broad Teifi washes alongside the beautifully-kept churchyard of Llandyfriog, the last recorded duel in Wales occurred in 1814 (SN 333412). This confrontation took place between Messrs. Beynon and Heslop. Both, it seems, were drinking (and probably drunk) in "The Salutation" pub at Newcastle Emlyn when Beynon questioned the chastity of the barmaid so precipitating a challenge from the gallant, if foolhardy Heslop. Pistols were chosen and it was agreed that each man would stand on either side of a stream, approach each other backwards and, after a prescribed number of paces, turn and fire. Either losing his nerve or wanting to steal a march on his adversary, Beynon turned early and shot the wretched Heslop in the back. It caused a tremendous sen-sation and provided a source of tap-room and dining-table gossip for many a month! History does not record the fate of Beynon, nor the reaction of the slighted barmaid. As for Heslop, he lies in Llandyfriog churchyard close to generations of Lloyds of Cilgwyn, his resting-place being marked with the simple inscription: "Alas poor Heslop".

From Llandyfriog the Teifi curls lazily through meadowland towards Newcastle Emlyn, yet another location traditionally associated with Vortigern. The site of the original castle of Emlyn, which we know to have been occupied by Llywelyn ap Iorwerth in 1215, has been identified to the north of the river, while the present scanty ruins overlie the "Newcastle" probably built by Maredudd ap Rhys around 1240. This in turn is thought to have occupied the site of an older promontory fort of the type commonly found on Teifiside[56]. A report on the condition of the castle in 1341 draws attention to the weakness of the walls and the unsteadi-ness of the drawbridge—so unsteady in fact that no horse would cross it. All this was rectified

Llandyfriog Church

49

"Alas; Poor Heslop"

Newcastle Emlyn: the Castle ruins

towards the end of the next century when the lucky Rhys ap Thomas, friend and benefactor of the usurper Henry Tudor, began to rebuild the place as a fortified mansion befitting his status as a great territorial magnate. The pair of entrance towers, along with the fragments of contiguous walling and grass-grown earthworks are of this period. Sir Rhys continued to thrive under Henry VIII, whom he accompanied on the invasion of France in 1513 and by whom he was created a Knight of the Garter. He eventually died in 1525 and following the execution of his grandson Rhys ap Gruffydd in 1531 (on a trumped-up charge which may have been fabricated on account of his vehement opposition to Anne Boleyn), the estates reverted to the Crown. Gruffydd's convenient attainder produced a windfall for the state coffers in the form of personal property valued at upwards of £30,000 together with £10,000 annually in rents and other charges on the estate. The castle in the meantime was granted to the influential Vaughan family of Golden Grove in Carmarthenshire who held it for the next hundred years or so. Richard Vaughan, earl of Carberry, garrisoned the place on behalf of the King during the Civil Wars and was obliged to endure a lengthy siege by Parliamentary forces under the command of General Laugharne. This was eventually lifted in 1644 by Sir Charles Gerrard, whose troops for good measure plundered Tregaron and Lampeter before marching to Newcastle Emlyn where they drove off the besiegers after heavy fighting in which 200 men died. The Teifiside locals, like many of their countrymen, were far too sensible to become embroiled in the factional blood-letting. In Pembrokeshire, for example, active participation in the Civil Wars seems to have been virtually confined to the Englishry, while the worthy burghers of Carmarthen were wise enough to surrender the town voluntarily to General Laugharne with effusive promises of loyalty to Parliament provided no harm were to come to them. Missing the point completely, one contemporary wrote, "The Welsh care not for fighting but upon passage, and scarce then either, except they have a good opportunity. For the Welsh have always been observed to be

Newcastle Emlyn

cowards and seldom act but upon advantage"[57]. In other words they preferred the tactics of the good guerilla fighter to the set piece battle.

Sir Rhys ap Thomas's great building was severely damaged during the course of Laugharne's siege and it was eventually abandoned in 1648, much of the stone and rubble of the walls being subsequently used for building houses in the town. The massive oak timbers were purloined by the Lloyd family for the construction of their mansion of Old Cilgwyn on the northern outskirts of Newcastle Emlyn and when this was replaced by the present Cilgwyn, an unfortunate late Victorian fancy with a rather bedraggled air about it, some of the old timbers were incorporated.

A typical little market town, Newcastle Emlyn is marvellously supplied with pubs and ex-pubs masquerading as houses. A century ago these catered for the scores of drovers and dealers who thronged the town on market days when horses and cattle lined the streets from Adpar to

Cilgwyn House

Aberarad. And the dealers still come to the flourishing modern market; men with craggy, weather-beaten faces thoughtfully scrutinising pens of cattle and sheep and unable to resist the temptation of poking a recumbent pig with a knarled stick. Times may have changed; yet in the cattle market one can still pick up that timeless atavistic whiff of cattle dung and damp fleeces which, mingled with that of peat-smoke and drying clothes, must have prevailed in the days when men and animals shared the same roof in the longhouse.

CHAPTER FOUR

Scholars and Gentlemen,
Coracles and Manufacturers;
Newcastle Emlyn to Cilgerran

As the road through the bustling streets of Newcastle Emlyn crosses the Teifi it runs into Adpar (Trerhedyn). Now little more than an outpost of Newcastle Emlyn, Adpar was formerly a chartered borough returning a member to Parliament, a privilege it retained until 1742 when the charter was revoked—allegedly because of certain irregularities involving the election of a member, but more probably because the borough failed to undertake its statutory corporate acts[58]. Set in the wall of a shop near the bridge over the Teifi, a plaque placed in 1912 by the "Committee of the Happy Winter Evening Entertainments" proclaims that close to this spot was located Wales's first official printing press. For centuries before 1700 the Teifi valley had played an important

rôle in the literary life of Wales, and with the relaxation of licensing laws and the limits imposed on the activities of Dissenters, there occurred a veritable renaissance in literary activity, predominantly of a religious nature. As Geraint Jenkins has demonstrated, the traditional passion for poetry and prose was now injected with a vigorous religious flavour which, ". . . galvanised Anglicans and Dissenters alike to sustain local printing presses in a bid to maintain those traditions and to foster the growth of literacy"[59]. Isaac Carter's press at Trerhedyn, active between 1718/19 and 1724, was to the forefront of this movement and continued to publish books following its removal to Carmarthen at the latter date. By tradition Carter's first publication was *Eglurhad o Gatechism Byrraf*

The Bridge at Cenarth: late 19th century

53

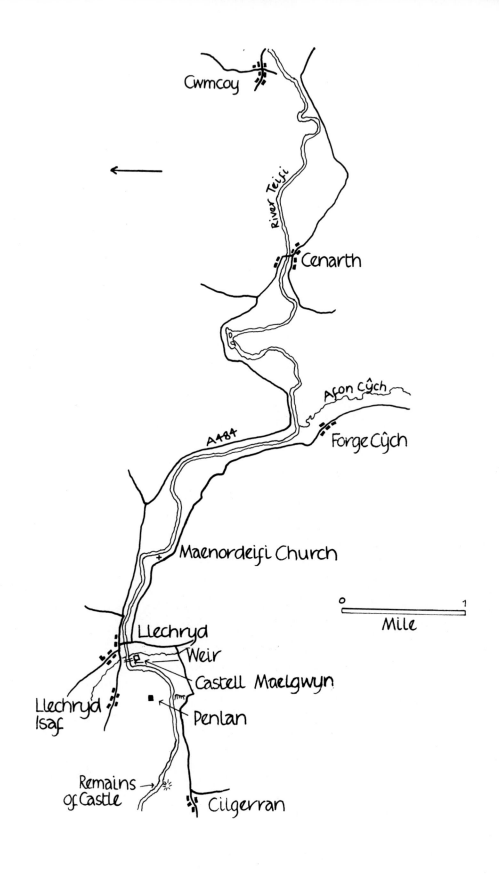

y Gymanfa (The Explanation of the Shortest Catechism of the Gymanfa) (1719) although *Can o Sen i'w hen Feistr Tobacco,* (An Insulting Song to his Old Tobacco Master) from the pen of Alban Thomas (d. 1740), cleric, translator and poet, appeared the year previously. Thomas, an important figure in the literary revival centred upon Newcastle Emlyn, worked on a number of projects with Carter, while his son, another Alban (1686-1771) was also deeply involved in literary matters. Sometime physician and librarian of the Ashmolean Museum, Alban Thomas junior returned to Wales under suspicion of Jacobite sympathies and worked with the great antiquary and wonderfully gifted scholar Moses Williams (1685-1742) in his stalwart, if only partially successful, attempts to preserve and publish Welsh manuscript material. Like all good antiquarian clerics, Williams remained alive to his pastoral responsibilities and in 1715 he published no fewer than 1000 Welsh catechisms for his Llanwenog parishioners[60].

It is not difficult to conjure up an image of these scholarly gentlemen wandering deep in animated conversation along the banks of the Teifi as it meanders through the meadows beyond Newcastle Emlyn, gradually gaining pace until, with quiet splendour, it runs headlong into a broad gorge towards Cenarth. A rocky path, worn smooth by generations of tourists skirts the base of the gorge where woods of oak and ash cling uneasily to the sides of bluebell-floored slopes. Here the pungent smell of honeysuckle and dogrose hangs on the air and high above the mew of a buzzard descants on the roar of the rapids above Cenarth bridge.

Since Giraldus Cambrensis described the rapids, or falls of Cenarth, late in the 12th century, they have continued to excite the interest of travellers, intrigued and fascinated by the way that salmon managed to negotiate them. Here is Michael Drayton writing in 1622:

"Here, when the labouring fish doth at the foot arrive,
And finds that by his strength but vainly he doth strive,
His tale takes in his teeth: and bending like a bow,
That's to the compass drawn, aloft himself doth throw;
Then springing at his height, as doth a little wand,
That bended end to end, and flerted from the hand,
Far off itself doth cast . . ."

Long before Giraldus's time the stretch of river between Cenarth and Cilgerran had been famed for its salmon of which many succumbed to the wiles of the Teifi coracle-men. The early coracles, in some features similar to the "curraghs" of Dark Age Irish settlers, were constructed of wicker-work and covered with tanned animal hides. Eventually, flannel dipped in a boiling mixture of tar and resin was used in preference to hide, this covering being placed on a framework of willow and hazel construction. Examples of these extraordinary and versatile craft are to be seen at the Welsh Folk Museum at St. Fagans, and at the excellent little fishing museum at Cenarth itself which also exhibits a whole range of ghoulish instruments of the fisherman's art. In the second half of the 18th century coracles were in daily use on the river and by 1861 it was estimated that over 300 were being worked on the Teifi with 28 pairs of coracle fishermen operating full-time above Llechryd bridge[61]. When the early 19th century antiquary Sir Richard Colt Hoare travelled by boat from Cardigan to Cilgerran (for which he grudgingly had to part with ten shillings) he noted that the coracles "add much to the animation of the views[62]. So convenient were these practical and easily-handleable craft that, "The fisherman, when his labour is over, flings his boat across his back, and marches homewards under the burden of his machine and booty. There is scarcely a cottage in the neighbourhood of the Tivy . . . without its coracle hanging by the door"[63]. For the coracle-men, salmon fishing provided the primary source of income with the river being divided into four sections fished respectively by the men of Cenarth, Abercuch, Llechryd and Cilgerran. Within the season, usually between August and February, fishing was conducted in a highly organised manner according to a code of rigid rules transmitted orally from father to son. But they

Cenarth

were not above letting their hair down from time to time and when annual coracle races were established in the 1830's under the patronage of a local gentleman, Lewis Gomer of Tymawr-y-Gwaith, there were usually over a score of entrants and many onlookers[64].

The right to fish without let or hindrance, held, "since time out of mind", was jealously guarded by the Teifi coraclemen who deeply resented the various Salmon Fisheries Acts of the 1860's which began gradually to encroach upon their activities. In fairness to the authorities, something had to be done to prevent serious over-fishing. When the Rev. John Evans travelled the area in 1805 he noted that the supply of salmon far exceeded local demand and that a great deal of fish was dried, salted and "exported" at 6d. per pound, being, as he put it, "an infallible remedy for a disordered appetite"[65]. But by the time Meyrick came to write his *History of Cardiganshire* in 1808 things had changed somewhat. Fifty years previously, he explained, a whole fish had sold for 1d.

whereas now, lack of restraint in the spawning season had so reduced supplies that one had to pay 6d.—1/- per pound for the privilege of eating fresh salmon[66].

To the chagrin of the coraclemen, the Salmon Fisheries Acts required them to take out licences. This they regarded as a contravention of their ancient rights, strongly suspecting that the legislation was a mere contrivance to allow gentlemanly pliers of the rod-and-line to catch more fish. Accordingly, when they met together on March 8th, 1867 they agreed, as a man, to cock a snook at the authorities by refusing to take out licences, believing that, ". . . the Fisheries Acts by which the present system of licences was created was not the law of the land but simply an arrangement among the gentry"[67]. But they could not kick against the pricks for long and were gradually forced to accede to the licensing arrangements. Inevitably, with the growth of tourism and increasing demand for sport from rod-and-line fishermen, further legislation was brought to bear so that by

1935 no further licences were issued to new fishermen in the river above Llechryd bridge and at present there is no official coracle fishing at Cenarth.

But the struggle continues. The remaining practitioners of the ancient craft have entered the lists against a bureaucratic leviathan in the form of the Welsh Water Authority. The latter is keen to prevent poaching, whether by means of the vertically-suspended gill net or the gaff. Illegal gaffing is generally carried out at night with the aid of a powerful torch, and the Authority has sought to ban night fishing, a course of action which would severely hamper the coracle-fishing trade since fish would easily avoid the readily visible trawl net if this could only be used during daylight hours. Happily, the coracle-men, in association with the seine nets-men of the Teifi estuary, have successfully resisted and the Authority has agreed to shelve the bye-law for the time being. Nevertheless, the proposal to reduce to twelve the number of coracle licences issued in 1986 may mean the beginning of the end of a long and largely honourable tradition.

On the river bank opposite the salmon leap at Cenarth stand the remains of a 17th century watermill, currently in the process of restoration. This probably occupies the site of the mill for which, in 1300, Walter de Pederton, Justiciar for West Wales, rendered account of 33/4 to King Edward I[68]. Like the four hundred year old Felin Geri mill at Cwm Coy in the unspoilt Ceri Valley, Cenarth Mill served the needs of the immediate locality and in a semi-subsistence economy was of vital local importance. Until well into the 19th century most of these mills were owned by the Lord of the Manor—Cenarth Mill being the property of the Cawdor Estate—and tenants were more-or-less compelled to take their corn to be ground at the lord's mill as opposed to anyone else's. In fact, many leases and tenancy agreements set out, in addition to cash rent payments, a whole range of "duties" expected of tenants. These might include delivering a specified number of

Cenarth Mill

chickens to the lord at Shrove-tide, providing several days' labour each year on his demesne and, almost inevitably, having one's corn ground at his mill. The survival of the latter "service rent" into the 19th century was a source of some grievance, especially when the mill itself had been leased by the lord of the manor to an outsider who enjoyed the right to levy toll on the ground corn[69]. Like the lessees of tollgates on the turnpike roads, these men were often in the business for the maximum gain and "screwed" their captive clientèle for as much as they possibly could. Take for example, Melin Rhydowen at Llandysul, let off by the Lord of the Manor in the early 17th century. Tenants regularly complained that the lessee of this mill claimed as a toll up to 1/6 of the corn ground, besides keeping for himself all the meal that adhered to the millstones—often as much as 5 toll dishes per milling. As if this were not enough, tenants were expected also to help with thatching the mill and scouring the millpond.

Many of those who grudgingly trundled their cumbersome carts towards the mill now rest in the churchyard of Cenarth, embracing the simple Victorian church high above the river. The building itself contains little of interest apart from an early font. This apparently, was thrown out by the Puritans and thence commenced a career as a pig trough or flower-bowl, from which indignities it was rescued in the last century and restored to its rightful place. Immediately opposite the south porch, a stone of Dark Age provenance commemorates Curneagus, son of Andagellus (*Cureagn 1 filii Andagell*). This was first identified and described by Lewis Morris, the famous Anglesey antiquary, when it stood on the roadside near Bwlch-y-Clawdd, Maenclochog, Pembrokeshire.

In a field beyond the White Hart pub, more-or-less within sight of the church, a motte castle of some 450 foot circumference lurks beneath a clump of trees. The surrounding ditch was originally of some depth but is now partially infilled by a combination of tree debris and earth eroded from the bank by cattle. In all likelihood the site is that mentioned in the Pipe Rolls on several occasions between 1184 and 1204, and might claim to share with Cilgerran Castle the

Standing stone; Cenarth churchyard

dubious honour of being one of the homes of Nest, daughter of Rhys ap Tewdwr, last king of Deheubarth[70]. The remarkable career of Nest is the very stuff of medieval romance and would have been given the full-blooded treatment by a Verdi or Donizetti had they had access to the story! Seduced and impregnated by Henry I (who had made her his ward in 1093 after her father's death), Nest was married off by the King to Gerald de Windsor, Constable of Pembroke, with whom she lived at the (unidentified) castle of Cenarth Bychan and by whom she had a child, Angharad, mother of Giraldus Cambrensis. Enter now a particularly bloodthirsty character in the form of Owain, son of Cadwgan, Prince of Powys, a typically medieval thug much-given to gouging out his enemies' eyes. Invited to spend Christmas at Cenarth Bychan, Owain, "at the instigation of the Devil", fell for Nest and attempted to abduct both her and her family after laying waste the castle[71]. Gerald managed to escape, but Owain grabbed Nest (who may not have been entirely unwilling), along with her two children and one of Gerald's natural off-spring. When he arrived with his prizes at his father's house at Llangollen, Owain found Cadwgan in a state of panic at the thought of the king's reaction to his son's excesses. After some pressure from his father, Owain released the children. But this gesture was not enough to pacify the enraged king who proceeded to grant most of Cadwgan's lands to his vassal Gilbert Fitz Richard, also, for good measure, giving him *carte blanche* to devastate much of Dyfed. Although Cadwgan was eventually restored to Henry I's favour, Owain remained a wanted man. He fled to Ireland, only to return several years later when, ironically, he was killed in battle by Gerald himself. Nest, meanwhile, survived and prospered and when Gerald died she married Gruffydd ap Rhys, thereby founding yet another princely line. The marital and sexual behaviour of this Welsh "Helen of Troy" caused chaos among the leading families of Wales and it may be no exaggeration to suggest that the resulting disunity helped considerably the Norman advance into the country.

Between Cenarth and Llechryd the river passes through well-cultivated farmland, its banks supporting otters and polecats and providing a breeding ground for kingfisher, mallard, sandpiper and wagtail. After Cenarth

The Teifi near Llechryd

the main river is joined by Afon Cuch at the end of a sublimely beautiful wooded valley haunted by the shades of the knights of the Mabinogion. Until the close of the 19th century, craftsmen occupying this little valley were renowned for their woodturning skills and for the quality of the clogs and household objects which they fashioned from the abundant stands of alder and

Llechryd Bridge (late 19th century), with a view of the Church of the Holy Cross

59

Maenordeifi Church

Maenordeifi Church

sycamore. Alder was an ideal timber for clog-making since it didn't readily split and could be easily shaped. Harvested when about 18 inches in diameter, the trees were split into logs and left to season for 9 months before being roughed into shape, dried in the open air and finally carved into clog bases. The sycamore, growing like a weed in the woods and hedgerows of West Wales, lent itself ideally to the manufacture of dairy utensils, plates, cheese casks and butter pats. It could be carved while still green, immersed in water without cracking and warping, did not taint food products, and readily absorbed dyes without obscuring the natural grain of the wood. Sycamore thus came to be widely used for making carved spoons and turned bowls, either for utilitarian purposes or, in the case of the highly-decorated love-spoons of the 18th and 19th centuries, as gifts or tokens. These love-spoons, some of them of remarkable complexity, were often carved on winter nights by local farmers and their families and provided a useful source of income when sold at the spring fairs and markets[72].

Before it creeps round the edge of the park of Castell Maelgwyn the Teifi passes the fine old church of Maenordeifi with its plain white-washed exterior, Celtic belltower, box pews and Tudor-style font (SN 229433). Included among the long list of Rectors inscribed on the wall of the church is David Phillips, Rector in 1680. Like many of his contemporaries, Phillips was an absentee who had abandoned his pastoral duties in favour of the fleshpots of London. According to a letter written in 1698 by the dignitaries of the parish to the Bishop of St. Davids, he had allowed the glebe buildings to fall into disrepair, and the surrounding meadows to become flooded, besides felling certain trees in the churchyard, "by the help of a nonconformist teacher and carpenter". Far worse, he had appointed as his curate, ". . . an insufficient and notorious person . . . who is the reputed father of several bastards which is a very ill example . . . and a cause of great scoff to all nonconformists". With the established church in such a state it is small wonder that Nonconformity gained a hold in West Wales and was thereby enabled to march so triumphantly through the following centuries.

The fine 19th century monuments to the Colbys of Ffynone and the Saunders-Davies's of Pentre inside Maenordeifi church and the high quality of monumental masonry in the church-yard bespeak a prosperous gentry and middle class. Indeed, as one progresses downriver, the quantity of ironwork enclosing the dead and the hyperbole of the language commemorating them seems to increase in direct proportion with the improving agricultural conditions. Not without reason did the founders of the houses of Cilgwyn, Coedmor, Pentre, Llangoedmor and the rest establish themselves in this rich Canaan of fertile meadows and exquisite landscape. As H. M. Vaughan remembered, in his fondly nostalgic book, *The South Wales Squires,* the lower Teifi Valley contained, in the balmy days of the 1890's, almost 50 country houses in an area of less than 100 square miles. Intermarrying and interbreeding, they formed a closely-knit society whose unity was born of a similarity of class and aspirations. They visited each other's houses in a carefully orchestrated social round, tore through the countryside with the Teifiside Foxhounds, drank tea, gossipped and flirted at the Newcastle Emlyn Tennis Club and danced, dined and tippled throughout the annual Hunt week[73].

The Teifiside Hunt was founded in 1736 and after going out of action during the American War of Independence and the Napoleonic Wars was revived in 1815 under the mastership of Captain Lewes of Llysnewydd. Gentlemen throughout South Wales rode with the hounds and probably turned out *en masse* on that celebrated day when "The First Gentleman of Europe", the Prince of Wales, and later George IV, graced the field with his ample presence. The Prince must have enjoyed himself since he later granted members of the Hunt the right to sport the *fleur de lys* on their brightly-polished buttons. The honour of the Hunt received a severe blow on the death of Queen Victoria in 1901 when, despite the Court's ordering of a month of mourning, the master, Captain E. W. Parry-Pryse of Neuadd Trefawr (and later Sir Edward

Pryse of Gogerddan), took the hounds into the field. Local loyalists were shocked. One outraged wit, signing himself "A Loyal Local and Disgusted Sportsman", penned a lengthy ditty condemning this insensitive act, and along with many highly-critical observations, he wrote:

"Then hasten, old comrades away,
  Our mourning we'll put off today;
  We'll think of our Queen, and all she has been
  Later on, but just now we can't stay . . ."[74].

By the 1890's, the sun was beginning to sink and the old way of life of the Teifiside gentry seemed inexorably to be drawing towards its close. Agricultural depression and mortgage commitments had dealt body-blows to the finances of landowners, their political hegemony had been finally shattered, and they no longer enjoyed the automatic and unquestioning loyalty of their tenants and dependants. The world was rapidly changing and following the sickening war of 1914-18 when sons and heirs were mown down in appalling numbers, many estates were sold and their previous owners left the Teifi valley with what remained of their diminished fortunes. H. M. Vaughan, himself a scion of Llangoedmor, observed with sardonic irony that few people regretted the passing of the old-style gentry, ". . . especially the peasants and the cottagers, who now benefit from the proverbial generosity of the profiteer and the get-rich-quick farmers, who are now the lords of the Teifi Valley"[75].

A linear depression in the meadows between Maenordeifi church and the Teifi marks the remains of an old canal which originally cut across the minor road to Llechryd, following the left hand side of this road as it approaches Castell Maelgwyn and thence under a bridge carrying an attractive cast iron plaque dated 1799 (SN 218436). The canal was originally cut to carry water from the Teifi and so to provide power for the tinplate works whose bedraggled remnants lie immediately behind Castell Maelgwyn. Canal construction apparently commenced sometime after 1772 when Walter Lloyd of Coedmor and his co-speculators in the tin-plate enterprise negotiated with William Harries, Rector of Maenordeifi, the right to drive a canal through the latter's glebelands. In consideration of a yearly rent of £2-10-0, to accrue from a 33 acre piece of land called "The Green Meadow", Lloyd and his heirs would enjoy access to their canal for all time[76].

The tinworks were originally operated by Walter Lloyd in partnership with William Dermer of London (carpenter), James Walker of Spitalfields (weaver) and Griffith Howell of London (slater)[77]. In March 1771, a few months after the articles of partnership had been drawn up Howell was in financial trouble having borrowed £1000 from Walker. Accordingly he agreed to assign to the latter his share of the capital and profits "in the weir, floodgates, forge, rolling mills and other buildings and works" by way of mortgage for securing the debt[78]. The tripartite partnership only lasted 7 years and was dissolved by the Court of Chancery in 1778 after which Walter Lloyd sold the enterprise to Messrs Halliday and Daniels for the considerable sum of £8250[79]. The sale was conditional upon the purchasers paying an annual rent of £52-10-0 for the privilege of taking water from the Teifi, a practice which limited the efficacy of the Lloyd's fish weir at Llechryd. Halliday and Daniels and subsequent owners of the works regularly attempted to renege upon this condition and the Coedmor family often resorted to law to recover their rent[80]. In 1794, for example, Thomas Lloyd paid the Carmarthen lawyer Herbert Lloyd £40-7-8 in respect of settlement of actions concerning the vexatious matter of the water-rent[81].

By this time, though, the works had passed to Sir Benjamin Hammett, a native of Taunton and sometime draper's assistant, who married a Cardiganshire girl before proceeding to make a modest fortune as a London banker[82]. In a move typical of a recently-arrived country gentleman, Hammett built Castell Maelgwyn, originally a nicely proportioned late 18th century house which managed to escape the worst excesses of Victorian embellishment only to fall prey to "improvements" upon conversion to an hotel in more recent years. After being shown round the works by Hammett's son, the traveller Warner was invited to dine in the house where he found,

". . . munificence, liberality and good humour; the charms of beauty and the attractions of female accomplishment"[83]. Warner and his contemporaries marvelled at the dynamism of Hammett's enterprise. Iron and raw materials were brought up-river from Cardigan on lighters pulled by horses treading a specially constructed towpath, and as the furnaces belched and the waterwheels creaked, some 300 men laboured to produce 12,000 tinplate boxes each year. The works ran profitably until the second quarter of the 19th century when Hammett's son, in a fit of pique after a dispute with the burgesses of Cilgerran, dismantled the operation and left the area.

In the closing years of the 18th century, Castell Maelgwyn must have been a bustling, noisy and rather smelly place. If the clatter of the tinplate works failed to disturb the repose of the house and its occupants, the Llechryd iron forge on the opposite bank of the river would have provided a less than desirable counterpoint[84]. The constant felling of trees for charcoal, the rush of water through leets and the incessant grind of machinery seem to have been too much for Sir Benjamin and when he secured the lease of the works from the Coedmor family he promptly dismantled them. The lease, of 100 years, was granted in 1792 by Thomas Lloyd and embraced the farm of Penlan Llechryd (81 acres) together with the limekiln and several other properties and included a clause allowing Hammett to pull down all existing structures[85]. So passed the Llechryd forge, active since the 17th century and a mere memory by the 1860's. No trace remains today[86].

Stretching across the river from the forge to the finely-crenellated stables of Castell Maelgwyn was the Llechryd fish weir whose ruins can still be seen protruding from the water in summertime. In times past weirs were common features of the Teifi and its tributaries, as witness the name-elements *gored* or *argae* (weir) and, particularly, *Pen-y-gored,* the original name of the Castell Maelgwyn site. Usually built to facilitate the efficient working of mill wheels, weirs were often so constructed that fish became stranded behind them and could thereby be trapped or gaffed with ease. The

authorities went to great lengths to put a stop to this practice but despite the strictures of the various Salmon and Freshwater Fisheries Acts of the 1860s it was not until the 1920's that legislation enforced approved "fish passes" on all dams and weirs associated with riverside mills. However, like the one at Cilgerran a mile or so downstream, the Llechryd weir was a *bona fide* fish weir, purpose-built of wood and stone following a grant by Queen Anne to the Lloyds of Coedmor[87]. Each year, once the salmon began to run up river in February, the Lloyds, mindful of profitable sales of smoked fish caught at the weir, commenced battle against unlicensed fishermen and legions of poachers. They cajoled, they threatened and they went to law; yet they could do little to prevent fish from being illicitly taken. Walter Lloyd, in 1785, offered bribes of half a guinea a time to witnesses against poachers and regularly sent out handwritten broadsheets warning locals of the terrible penalties that would befall any man taking fish without the permission of the estate office[88]. Moreover, he objected to *bona fide* coracle fishermen pulling their craft onto his riverside lands and, ". . . trod down the Grain and Hay growing on the same"[89]. The estate was adamant in enforcing this petty restriction and when T. E. Lloyd, M.P. leased the stone quarries near Fforest in 1878 it was clearly specified that the tenants should take every possible measure to prevent fishermen drying their nets on the quarry grounds[90]. The coracle-men were incensed. Writing to Lloyd on their behalf, one John Michael requested that coracle-owners could continue with this apparently harmless practice, promising that nets would not be hung on, ". . . any Tree or any growing thing which might be construed to be against your interests". In the same letter Michael observed that as quarry waste had now obscured the public path and lowered the level of the river, fishermen were prevented "from following strictly our legitimate mode of fishing". None of this would have cut much ice with Lloyd, who was privately hoping to get rid of the coraclemen once and for all and perhaps for this reason was quite happy to loan his boat to the official waterkeepers partolling the river on the lookout for anyone infringing fishing regulations. In what may have been a veiled warning Michael wrote, "We have always looked up to you as a Superior in the Neighbourhood and still do so, but we hoped we should never have occasion to associate any act of yours with those of Water Bailiffs and Police-men in the purusit of humble and industrious people . . ."[91].

"Water Bailiffs and Policemen" had been around since 1818 when the predecessor to the Salmon Fisheries Acts found its way to the Statute Book. The "Act for preventing the Destruction of the Breed of Salmon and Fish of the Salmon Kind in the Rivers of England" set out close seasons and specified the types of fish to be caught along with the legal mode of catch-ing them. Under the Act, J.P.s were given wide powers to appoint conservators as they felt fit and local Lords of the Manor were *required* to ensure the protection of rivers flowing through their properties. The house of Coedmor, whose ultimate objective seems to have been to gain sole rights to fishing on the Teifi, acted assidu-ously and came down heavily on anyone not fishing "by ancient right" or under the licence of the estate. Isaac Griffiths and Griffith Griffith, both of Llechryd, would have had every cause to feel apprehensive when they appeared, in 1818, before Thomas Lloyd of Coedmor in his capacity as a Justice of the Peace. Lloyd fined each of them £5 for contravening the 1818 Act (an enormous sum at the time when a farm labourer's weekly wage was 7/-), and it is not difficult to imagine the general nature of their conservation as they shuffled out of the doors of Coedmor mansion![92]. Among the Coedmor papers is an innocent-looking document written in a neat scribe's hand and entitled, "Expenses attending the preservation of the River". Cover-ing the years 1826 and 1827 and including dis-bursements by the estate under the 1818 Act, it details payments to "river watchers", payments to constables for escorting prisoners to gaol, and bribes (?) doled out to witnesses against poachers. This single sheet of paper speaks volumes about the tensions which must have prevailed on Teifiside at the time, a decade or so before the eruption of the Rebecca Riots. What personal dramas led to 1/- being given to Abel

Morris on New Year's Day 1827, ". . . for giving evidence respecting the firing of guns at the Watchman on the night of 25th Dec."! What sort of old scores were being settled when, a few days later, a shilling each in their hands, John Thomas and James John returned from Cardigan where they gave "evidence respecting the two coracles and net taken on the night of the 6th inst., the persons fishing with them having run away"![93]

By the early 1840's the lease of the Llechryd weir was held from Coedmor by Abel Lewis Gower, successor to the Hammetts at Castell Maelgwyn and a director of the Bank of England. Gower must have rued the day he came to Llechryd since his tenure of Castell Maelgwyn and the fish weir coincided with the anguished years of the Rebecca Riots. Local people had little taste for salmon, yet the rioters saw fish weirs as symbols of oppression and in the specific case of Llechryd, which prevented fish from moving upriver except in times of flood, as a means of adversely affecting the livelihood of fishermen at Cenarth and elsewhere. Hence they decided to destroy it. After repeated threats and warnings to Gower a great crowd assembled on the 17th century bridge on July 18th, 1844 and launched an attack on the weir. They failed to do much damage on this occasion but succeeded a couple of months later despite the presence of 25 soldiers and 12 London police-men hired by Gower for his protection. Rather half-heartedly a disgusted Gower rebuilt the weir, only to see it pulled down once again. Enough was enough; he abandoned the broken structure to the river and the forces of decay[94].

Excessive, and often unnecessary, toll pay-ments levied on turnpike roads was a major source of irritation for country people of whom many would have secretly applauded the arson and vandalism of the Rebecca Rioters. Not least among the rioters' covet supporters were the farmers who resented having to pay heavy tolls on loads of lime, and those waiting patiently by the limekiln on the Cardiganshire side of the river near the modern sewage works beyond Llechryd Isaf would doubtless have approved of the destruction of the weir (SN 212439). This large kiln of late 18th or early 19th century type provided lime for the tin and iron forges as well as for agricultural purposes, and is probably the descendant of the one mentioned in the articles of sale of the iron forge in 1751 which included a limekiln "lately built and erected". It is currently overgrown and surrounded by rubbish and barbed wire, its flanking walls sprouting ash and sycamore. A structure deserving of conservation, perhaps?

According to Meyrick's *History of Cardiganshire*, the vault of the Lloyds of Coedmor is to be found in the Church of the Holy Cross at Llechryd. Being keen to find the burial place of such a celebrated local family, founders, among other things, of the first Independent chapel in the Teifi Valley, I fought my way around a churchyard virtually overgrown with an almost impenetrable tangle of brambles. Eventually I reached the door of the ivy-clad ruin of the church to be greeted by a "Danger" notice advising me to go no further. Inspired less by bravery than curiosity, I managed to get into the church which comprises an undivided nave and chancel, a south chapel and contains softwood box pews. The Church was partially restored by local enthusiasts in the 1930's, Communion being celebrated there on June 18th, 1933[95]. It has now been deconsecrated: presumably it will eventually be sold and converted to secular use, when the old gravestones will probably be arranged round the perimeter of the churchyard with soulless efficiency. The church, overlooking the River Teifi, was apparently renovated in the 1840's, ". . . through the exertions of the incumbent"[96]. But his efforts were not enough and it was abandoned in 1879, being replaced by the undistinguished St. Tydfil's built at the top end of the village and consecrated in 1878[97].

St. Tydfil's was financed by public subscription organised, for the most part, by Eliza Webley Parry of Glanhelyg in her capacity as secretary to the committee of local gentry who had taken it upon themselves to build a new parish church. By 1877 the committee had collected £700, a sum falling rather short of the accepted tender

The Church of the Holy Cross, Llechryd

of £995-5-0 submitted by the builders, John Thomas of Llwyncelyn and Thomas Lewis of Newcastle Emlyn who were to effect the work according to the plans of Mr. Middleton, the architect. Fortunately a fairy godmother appeared in the form of Maria Brigstocke of Blaenpant who agreed to pay the balance of the money along with a further £100 to be used for building an appropriate enclosure and gateway for the new church[98].

Flowing beneath Llechryd bridge and beyond the stables of Castell Maelgwyn, the River Teifi runs deep and silent through the majestic Cilgerran Gorge. The Cardiganshire side of the gorge boasts marvellous natural woodlands, the remains of the great medieval forest of Ceredigion Iscoed, gradually whittled away first by charcoal burners and then by timber traders providing materials for ship-building in Cardigan and elsewhere. Shipbuilding absorbed enormous quantities of timber and those few lone Elizabethan voices who warned of the dangers of felling too many oaks in Ceredigion Iscoed would have been shocked to learn that to build a single 120 gun 3-decker of the sort common in Nelson's day required no less than 75 acres of mature oak forest. Today sessile oaks dominate a mixture of species forming a rich habitat for mammals and birds and, for those with an interest in the less obvious of nature's marvels, a splendid flora of epiphytic lichens.

The opposite side of Cilgerran Gorge comprises a woodland of relatively young beech and sycamore, the older trees having disappeared in the face of slate and flagstone quarrying in the 18th and 19th centuries. Steep cliff faces and the overgrown and fern-sprouting ruins of abandoned quarry buildings combine with tall trees and thick scrub to yield a different, but equally interesting habitat to that of the older woodlands across the river. Here badgers and foxes thrive, otter and mink haunt the river bank and birds of all descriptions dart among the trees. Due largely to the encouragement of the Lloyds of Coedmor, a good deal of the gorge between Castell Maelgwyn and the marshes above Cardigan was exploited for slate or flagstones. Small-scale 18th century workings steadily expanded so that by the middle of the next

century quarrying was a major source of local employment with six quarries supporting upwards of 100 people by 1867[99]. Slates and slabs were conveyed downriver on lighters to Cardigan whence they were shipped to the ports of the Bristol Channel, northwards to Aberystwyth and, on occasions, across the Celtic Sea to Waterford, Wicklow and Dublin[100].

Like most extractive industries, slate quarrying yielded undesirable by-products, in this case thousands of tons of dross, dumped for generations on the Pembrokeshire bank of the Teifi. Inevitably this affected the flow of the river and when the county surveyor James W. Szlumper surveyed the situation in 1873 he found that despite attempts to build retaining walls, not only had the riverbed been progressively raised but the width of the channel had declined from over 100 feet in 1800 to a mere 28 feet. This was a serious matter and had led to extensive flooding of the Teifi valley above Llechryd. Szlumper suggested that the problem could be resolved by laying a tram-way along the river bank by which the rubble could be removed and subsequently dumped on the Cardigan marches. This proposal seems to have been put into effect, the short stretch of track providing a useful bonus by way of a convenient means of transport of limestone, coal and culm from Cardigan to Cilgerran[101].

The tramway is specifically mentioned in the 14 year lease of the Raven and Lower Quarries on Fforest Farm, granted by T. E. Lloyd to David Sambrook and David Owens, quarrymen, in 1878 (SN 188439). The terms of the lease forbade the quarrymen from depositing spoil on the farm or in the bed of the river and granted them permission to construct a riverside wharf (whose remains are still visible) together with a road across Rosehill Farm to be used solely for the transport of quarried stone. On its part the Coedmor estate was to enjoy an annual rent of £60 (rising to £70 upon the completion of the Crymych to Cardigan railway link) and the right to purchase building materials from the partnership at a 5% discount[102].

Cilgerran shares with Llechryd a long tradition of salmon fishing and numerous medieval documents testify to the mechanism whereby the Crown granted leases of fisheries to local dignitaries who were thereby enabled to let out fishing rights to their tenants. In 1427, for example, the fishery between Cilgerran and Newcastle Emlyn was leased by the Crown to Rhys ap Dafydd ap Thomas of Llandysul for a yearly rent of 4/- which he was able to recoup many times over by sub-letting[103]. 150 years later Elizabeth I granted the same stretch of water to Richard Gwynne on a 21 year lease in consideration of 4/- payable annually at the feast of St. Michael the Archangel[104]. Gwynne seems to have given up his lease within a few years since in 1596 one Richard Mortymer became the lessee and granted David Price the right to fish the pool of Pwll y Rhydhir with various types of nets but not with "corrogles" or "any new devices or engines"[105]. Gwynne was succeeded as lessee by James Lewes of Abernantbychan who, by Letters Patent of 1633, also enjoyed the right of tolls of the fair of Cardigan, taking place on the Feast of the Holy Trinity[106].

The fish weir at Cilgerran, marking the beginning of the stretch of water mentioned in the documents cited above, was located at the foot of the rocky eminence occupied by Cilgerran Castle, a little above the point where the Plysgog stream joins the Teifi (SN 195433). Constructed of stone and timber and described by George Owen of Henllys as ". . . the chiefest weare of all Wales", this was an ancient edifice even in Elizabethan times. An earlier weir had proved an inconvenient obstacle to boats conveying building material from Cardigan to Cilgerran Castle and had been dismantled on the orders of Edward I. In 1314, however, the weir was leased to John de Hastings who rebuilt it in such a way that ships carrying oaks from the forest of Coedmor could readily negotiate it as they sailed downriver to Cardigan[107]. The weir, of course, required constant repair and a Commission reporting on the desecration of the Coedmor Forest during the reign of James I noted that ten mature oaks were annually required for the purpose. The clearance or even threat of clearance of woodlands for agriculture today can be guaranteed to spark off a flood of correspondence in the press and a raising in the collective blood-pressure of the conservationist lobby. But the loss of reserves of timber was as much a live issue in Jacobean times as it is in the 1980's. In 1621, the King's Forester petitioned the Court of the Exchequer regarding the felling of timber and clearance of woodland in the Forest of Coedmor. In their enthusiasm to create land for corn-growing, local people were alleged to have caused damage to the value of £3000 and, alarmingly, to have threatened to cut off the arms and legs of the King's Forester. Although the Court took the view that the petitioner had overstated his case and that in fact encroachment on the forest had been limited to the collection of scrubwood for domestic fires, the case, and the time and effort taken over it, emphasises the extent of the authorities' concern. A century later the Lloyds of Coedmor were regularly felling forests to serve the local tin and iron enterprises and in 1792, for example, Thomas Lloyd sold the timber on Fforest Farm to Sir Benjamin Hammett and his partners Alexander Raby and Thomas Cox, for £1500[108].

From medieval times the village of Cilgerran enjoyed the right to hold two livestock fairs; on June 13th and August 21st. These were occasions of great civic pomp with the town clerk and twelve officials parading through the village in their finery on the morning of the fair as a prelude to reading a proclamation itemising the level of tolls payable on goods sold. The town clerk's proclamation also announced the proscription of all offensive weapons and that any man, apart from the portreeve, sheriff and his officers, who carried arms during the course of the fair, did so at the risk of spending time in the stocks[109]. By the 19th century this and other ceremonies had been largely forgotten, yet the fairs continued to be major events in the social and commercial calendar. And what momentous occasions they were! Hundreds flocked to the village: farmers in pursuit of profit; labourers in pursuit of pleasure; girls in pursuit of boys and pickpockets in pursuit of whatever came their way. When the Rev. John Evans visited Cilgerran on a fair day in the early 1800's he estimated that some 20,000 cattle were on sale, ". . . though this was considered but a small fair". Not only were all the fields within 3 miles of the village stocked

Cilgerran Fair: late 19th century

with cattle awaiting buyers, but the inns were so full that Evans had to press on to Llechryd in order to get a bed for the night[110].

For more than seven centuries the fairs of Cilgerran and the daily life of the straggling village were overlooked by the castle standing majestically on its eminence high above the Teifi. Virtually unassailable from the west and north due to the deep gorge, the castle was ideally placed to control river traffic and to overawe the surrounding countryside. The Marcher Lordship of Cilgerran, established by Henry I, was first held by Gerald of Windsor, though whether he occupied a castle at Cilgerran is far from certain. Taking advantage of the years of anarchy following the death of Henry I, the Lord Rhys re-established the ancient kingdom of Deheubarth which embraced much of this part of South Wales, but when he died in 1197 his sons squabbled fatally among themselves thereby allowing the Normans, under William Marshall, earl of Pembroke, once more to gain a foothold and to capture Cilgerran. Marshall, in turn, was driven out by Llywelyn the Great who was himself displaced by Marshall's brother, another William. This was the end of the to-ing

and fro-ing and by 1223 Marshall was in complete control and he immediately set about remodelling the castle whose remains stand today. Henceforth Cilgerran would never again fall under long-term Welsh control and throughout the rest of the medieval period it maintained its status as an independent lordship, passing successively to a series of Marshall heirs and heiresses until it came into the possession of John de Hastings in 1273. The Hastings family, whose descendants became earls of Pembroke, held Cilgerran for most of the 14th century, long after the castle had begun to fall into disrepair. Some rebuilding was carried out towards the end of Edward III's reign in response to the threat of a French invasion, but much of this work was severely damaged in 1405 when the castle was briefly held by supporters of Owain Glyndŵr. The subsequent history of the castle is one of steady, but inexorable decay. The Vaughan family, to whom it was granted by Henry VII when the earldom of Pembroke reverted to the Crown, seem to have neglected the building and it slowly mouldered into a romantic ruin, the delight of 19th century travellers who scrambled up the stern towers to view the glories of the Teifi several hundred feet below. The same dramatic prospect can still be enjoyed[111].

Looking across the Teifi from the castle it is possible to pick out, among the ranks of ancient oaks and sprawling rhododendrons, the cupola and stuccoed front of Coedmor (SN 195435). Originally the fief of the Lords of Iscoed, the Coedmor estate passed, by way of the Montgomerys of Chirk, to the Lloyd family whose property it remained for more than 300 years. Typical of their class, the Lloyds had few pretentions to national prominence and throughout their long association with Coedmor produced no-one who stamped his personality indelibly upon the political or social scene. Nevertheless, they played a distinguished role in the history of the Teifi Valley, spawning a variety of men noted for their character if not necessarily for their virtue. Thomas Lloyd, for example, flourishing in the late 18th century, was a staunch Whig and Lord Lieutenant of the County whose dedication to his official pursuits was paralleled only by his enthusiasm for the bottle and his performance in the bedchamber. He sired numerous bastards who were generally put to work as servants in the mansion, their mothers being given farms or holdings on the estate at nominal rents. Curiously, the old squire's legitimate sons were treated rather less favourably, being sent out to labour on local farms as a means of saving the expense of educating them. Lloyd finally yielded to family pressures and agreed to send his eldest legitimate son to Rugby where the boy developed a taste for scholarship and politics. He was eventually to become the last Tory M.P. for the county of Cardigan, defeating the Liberal, E. M. Richards in 1874 and holding his seat until 1880. This Thomas E. Lloyd occupied the present mansion, replacing an older building whose walled gardens still survive a mile to the west. The mansion was a focal point for Teifiside society who flocked there for hunt meetings, soirées, croquet afternoons and other such innocent diversions. The list of guests at the ball held in October 1874 reads like a gazetteer of county families. Eighty people (with ladies outnumbering gentleman) danced to the strains of

Cilgerran Castle

Messrs Jones of Carmarthen's quadrille band, ate a hearty supper at 11.30 p.m., and wearily took to their carriages at 2 in the morning[112]. This sort of event presented the inevitable fire risk and like so many of Cardiganshire's country houses, Coedmor was threatened by flames on at least one occasion. On October 14th, 1916 the stabling and outbuildings were gutted, the mansion itself being spared thanks to the strenuous efforts of the men of Cilgerran who crossed the Teifi in their coracles to help quell the blaze. They were rewarded with a gift of £40 from a grateful Thomas Lloyd[113].

Like the graves of the Lloyds in Llechryd churchyard, the early 19th century house has been abandoned following the departure of the Lloyd heir to his properties in Africa. The stucco is peeling, the window frames are rotting, grass grows through the paved terrace and the lawns are overgrown with knapweed and thistle. In the elegant stable block with its dairy, horse boxes and pig-sties, doors hang drunkenly from their hinges and the delicate latticed windows are steadily losing their panes. The house has little in the way of architectural merit, yet it remains as a tangible reminder of a way of life now irretrievably lost and for that reason alone is deserving of preservation.

CHAPTER FIVE

The Lower Reaches;
Cilgerran to the Sea

In the gorge far below Coedmor the Teifi continues its stately progress towards the sea. Half-a-mile downriver, on the opposite side to the empty mansion is Fforest, a substantial farmhouse standing in view of Cilgerran Castle among a fine set of (sadly neglected) 19th century outbuildings. Beneath the farm buildings to the northwest of the present house lurk the remains of an earlier building of which the earliest recorded owner was Thomas Phaer (1510?–1560), M.P., Doctor of Medicine, Solicitor to the Council of the Marches, legal scholar, classicist and poet. Among Phaer's many literary achievements were included translations of the first nine books of The Aeneid (1558) and contributions to "A Mirror for Magistrates", that extraordinary collection of "historical" poems used extensively as source material by Shakespeare. Patronage from the Marquess of Winchester ensured Phaer a steady income from sinecures so that he was able to devote most of his time to literary and medical projects. A translation into English of the medieval didactic poem *Regimen Sanitatis Salerni* was followed by translations of French texts dealing with avoidance and treatment of the plague, and contributions to the celebrated "Book of Children". In this work he commended breast feeding, and discussed almost forty children's disorders ranging from squinting to "Pissing in the Bedde", offering, in each case, the usual bizarre remedies![114]

Tradition has it that Fforest was occupied by Parliamentary forces during the Civil Wars, the house being used as a base for bombarding Cilgerran Castle with cannon. In support of the tradition, Phillips, in his *History of Cilgerran* (1867), writes of earthworks in the field below the present house, "yet known and called by the name of 'Bulwark'," behind which the Cromwel-

Coedmor from Cilgerran Castle

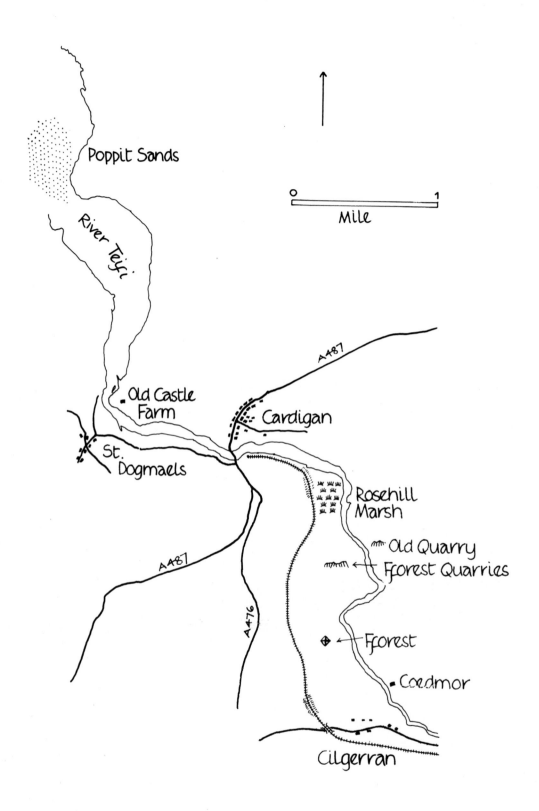

Poppit Sands

River Teifi

Old Castle Farm

St. Dogmaels

A487

Cardigan

A487

A476

Rosehill Marsh

Old Quarry
Fforest Quarries

Fforest

Coedmor

Cilgerran

0   1
Mile

Fforest

lian soldiers sheltered as they charged their weapons. I have found no such earthworks, no reference to 'Bulwark' on the local Tithe schedules nor any evidence to substantiate Phillips' claim that human bones and cannon balls were unearthed in the field. In fact, the tradition is a highly dubious one since Cilgerran Castle, unlike those of Newcastle Emlyn and Pembroke, seems to have played little part in the Wars.

Beyond the overgrown quarry-rubble forming much of the south bank of the Teifi downstream from Fforest, the river emerges from Cilgerran gorge at its confluence with the Pilau stream. In 1885 the dumping of rubble in the marshes and along the river bank was finally banned and as quarrying declined so a forlorn dross of grey waste was left behind. After a century of colonis-ation an interesting habitat has emerged from this unpromising raw material, with brambles, gorse and dogrose supporting many species of birds and offering cover to small mammals. The alder carr and freshwater marshes of Rosehill managed to survive the effects of largely uncon-trolled waste dumping and now offer a rich niche for the usual variety of mammals and birds along with the rare, strange and rather sinister water rail. The abandoned railway line skirting Rosehill Marsh and following the river bank to Cardigan harbours a flourishing adder popu-lation while the reed-grown salt marshes near the town yield a haven for waterfowl. Here, the rhythm of the tides dominates life, and the comings and goings of the fauna of this stretch of the river and of the nearby Cardigan Wildlife Park are authoritatively described in M. E. Baines's admirable *Guide to the Wildlife of the Teifi Estuary*. To the present author, passing through this fragile environment by way of the redundant railway line to Cardigan town, it seemed harshly ironic that in August 1985 the platform of the old station at the end of the line was piled high with drums of agro-chemicals.

Until the end of the Civil Wars the borough of Cardigan was dominated by the brooding presence of the castle, standing on its prominent site overlooking the Teifi. However, several generations before this castle came into being, Norman troops, probably under the command of Roger de Montgomery, built a fortress several

The Teifi beyond Cilgerran

The Teifi near Rosehill

hundred yards downriver on the north bank close to Oldcastle Farm (SN 164464). This was a relatively simple structure, a deep ditch having been dug in order to cut off a rocky river promontory upon which a motte was constructed. The site is now overgrown, the ditch serving as an outflow for farm sewage and other noisome effluents. Documentary references to a castle at Cardigan between the late 11th and early 13th centuries distinguish between defensive structures at Aberteifi and Cardigan with the older promontory fort regularly changing hands in the 12th century according to the relative ebb and flow of Welsh and Anglo-Norman fortunes. With the recognition, after his ultimate triumph by about 1165, of Rhys ap Gruffydd as tributary prince of Ceredigion, the castle came under Welsh control for the best part of a century before being re-taken by the English in the person of William Marshall. In 1240 he commenced the task of remodelling the "new" castle in stone and the formidable bastion appears to have been completed by 1295, being sufficiently well-appointed to accommodate Edward I in June of that year when he delivered the town's first charter.

A township had begun to develop around the castle several generations previously, and following the granting of the charter, the burgeoning settlement was occupied increasingly by Englishmen who were granted extensive trading rights and concessions, not the least of which was the right to trial by "English burgesses and true Englishmen". This privilege, along with burgess status, was denied the indigenous population who disapproved of the "plantation" of a semi-fortified English community and it is hardly surprising that the latter suffered from time to time, from "the malice of the Welsh". By the sixteenth century the town had outgrown its original walls and had extended into the area around St. Mary's Church and the jumble of little streets based on the Strand.

The castle, meanwhile, had already begun to decay and when John Speed produced his map of Cardigan in 1610 he described it as being, ". . . built upon a rock, both spacious and faire, had not stormes impaired her beauty, and time left her carkase a very Anatomie". The end finally came in the Civil Wars when the place was so devastated that little remained apart from the curtain wall and two flanking towers. A Georg-

Limekiln on the Teifi estuary

ian villa came eventually to be built on the site, the debris of the ruined towers and battlements being used as its foundations, and the castle dungeons as its cellars. The latter can still be seen, although the dilapidated villa has fallen prey to rising damp and wet-rot, its elderly owner living without electricity and sanitation in a nearby caravan accompanied by many cats and generations of ghosts. Ivy and virginia creeper have overtaken the mansion, windows have been broken, roofs have collapsed and the beds of begonia, lobelia and other ornamentals described by observers earlier this century have long given way to a morass of sycamore, bramble and scrub.

Cardigan Castle was well-placed to oversee the bridge across the Teifi and to protect the interests of the burghers and merchants whose warehouses mushroomed in the shadow of its walls. Small-scale coastal trading had been a vital facet of Cardigan's economy since medieval times and as trade expanded so did the quayside grow in importance. French wines and other exotic products had long been offloaded in the little harbour—to the delectation of the rich and privileged—but by the late 17th century the port had become a major centre for the export of corn, both to other points along the Welsh coastline and further afield to Bristol, Plymouth, Liverpool and London[115]. Concurrently the herring fishing industry was expanding and the quayside warehouses echoed to the lilt of Irish brogue as ships from across the Celtic sea discharged their cargoes of nets, casks and salt, all essential for preserving the herring catch. Salted herring not consumed locally might then be exported to Ireland, North Wales or mainland Europe. For this particular trade salt was required in vast quantities and in 1700, for example, no less than 4290 bushels were brought into Cardigan from Liverpool alone. Early 18th century legislation exempted fish-curers from the excise duty payable on salt, and customs officials strove to make sure that curers used their salt for *curing* and nothing more. The British have always been a scandalously over-taxed people and it is pleasant to record that the time-honoured craft of tax evasion was alive and well among the fish-curers of 18th century Cardigan. Thus, in 1737 the local customs officer attempted (unsuccessfully) to persuade J.P.s to issue summonses against David Phillips, John Jenkins, Barbara Evans and William Ackers for misappropriating salt delivered to them duty-free for curing purposes[116].

Like tax evasion, smuggling is an age-old occupation. In former times it assumed heroic proportions and few parts of the coastline of Britain could not boast a healthy population of smugglers drawn from all classes of society. The deeply-indented seaboard of Cardiganshire with its numerous inlets and concealed coves was ideally suited to illicit trading in brandy, tobacco, salt and other taxed commodities, and proved a fertile ground for the smuggler. Excisemen had a hard time of it since every man of spirit, from the shepherd to the squire and the joiner to the J.P., enjoyed the heady risks involved in smuggling. Seamen were regular habitués and Cardigan port must have thronged with smugglers like the crew of "The Charming Molly". Operating out of Cardigan, this 32 ton sloop was seized by the Chester customs authorities in 1767 on the grounds that she was carrying out an "illicit trade". But perhaps to no-one's surprise, she was handed back to her captain and crew following the intercession of certain influential gentlemen who may themselves have been beneficiaries of this unidentified but no doubt nefarious trade[117].

Smugglers apart, the inns and dives of Cardigan quayside were the haunts of cutpurses, prostitutes and all manner of exotic foreigners. Looking up from their glasses and peering down-river towards the estuary they would see the long prows of ships bringing in imports of seed-corn, tallow and limestone, meeting in mid-stream perhaps, craft heavily-laden with Cilgerran slate, Cardigan ale, bark from the oaks of Coedmor, or Teifi salmon headed for the tables of the Irish gentry. Maritime trade was Cardigan's life-blood, to which the merchants' houses in Quay Street and the remnants of the wharfs and warehouses on the river bank and the Mwldan bear silent witness.

Linked inextricably with coastal and international trade was the local shipbuilding industry which reached its apogee in the mid

Cardigan

19th century, incidentally wreaking havoc with the great oaks of Coedmor Forest and elsewhere. Landowners hard-pressed for cash lost little time in selling off their woodlands to both tanners and shipbuilders, a practice causing widespread concern since the rate of replanting lagged far behind the rate of felling. In a passage as relevant in 1986 as it was in 1804, the Rev. John Evans complained bitterly about the net loss of oaks on local estates, pointing out to their owners that as *patres patriae*, ". . . they have not only social duties to perform, but also duties to posterity"[118]. Evans' remarks struck a hollow note with gentlemen desperate to raise funds to support life styles well beyond the scope of their incomes and as Teifi timber became increasingly scarce, shipbuilders turned to Canada and Scandinavia for raw materials. By 1877, when the last major sea-going vessel was built at Cardigan, imported timber was almost exclusively used, with Canadian and Norwegian vessels regularly sailing up the estuary to discharge their cargoes at the Merchantile Wharf on the bank of the Teifi below Cardigan Bridge[119].

As trade grew, so was the harbour improved and by the turn of the 18th century it was able to give berth to ships of up to 250 tons displacement. Moreover, some 292 ships totalling 10,000 tons were registered in Cardigan by the 1820's, being serviced by 3 foundries, 3 sail-lofts and a chain and anchor factory. A casual look at the gravestones in the churchyard of St. Mary's, where ropemakers, sailmakers, shipbuilders and master mariners moulder in profusion, brings home vividly the importance of marine activity to the well-being of Cardigan. In common with those operating out of other ports in West Wales, most of Cardigan's ships were "share-owned", farmers being among the principal shareholders. Thus, when the 40 ton sloop "Denia" was sold in 1810, a 5/8 share was purchased for £395-15-0 by Thomas James, Mathias Mathias and Evan Evans, farmers[120]. Some years later the "Heart of Oak" was sold by the trustees of Thomas Jones (farmer), with 16/64 shares of the vessel being purchased for £80 by the timber merchants John Grainger and Robert Evans[121]. Several local farmers enjoyed an interest in the 87 ton brig "Renown", built in Cardigan in 1816. Under the captaincy of David Julian, this little vessel regularly ran up the north-west coast of Britain and crossed the Celtic sea with cargoes of salt, iron, coal, tin and bark. On one epic journey in 1824 she left Cardigan and made her way, via the Baltic Sea, to Russia, an odyssey whose details would have echoed around the pubs of Teifiside for many a month[122].

Despite all this activity and enterprise, Cardigan town failed to impress discerning travellers, especially those in pursuit of the "picturesque". Lipscomb, a hardened cynic whose views of matters Welsh were usually less than charitable, objected to the widespread Cardigan practice of varnishing the doors of houses with blood and was quite appalled by "the hideous custom of whitewashing". This, he believed, should be abolished, since, " . . . it offends the eye by a glare highly unpleasant; destroys the harmony of the picture . . . and impoverishes the prospect"[123]. Malkin, a man concerned with more commonsense matters, complained of the "meanness" of Cardigan. "The shops are mean and apparently ill-supplied. I have so far personal experience upon

which to found my judgement, that this country town could not furnish me with a pair of ready-made shoes of which I stood sorely in need". Yet, though he found the interior of the town to be indifferently built and wearing an air of poverty, he did at least concede that the commercial buildings "about the edge of the water" were not without interest[124].

In the fifty years before Malkin's visit, the face of Cardigan had changed considerably. St. Mary's Church had been extensively rebuilt in 1748 following the collapse of the tower in 1705, numerous wharfs had appeared on the quayside, Nash had remodelled Cardigan Priory in 1792 and, as if to remind us of the darker side of the "Age of Reason", the Corporation had set aside a spot near the Shire Hall, "for the burning of Malefactors"[125]. Among the more substantial buildings was Nash's rather grim gaol, completed in 1793. The goal and its associated exercise yard stood on the spot at the end of the High Street now occupied by Stanley House and the Highbury and Belmont Hotels, the latter standing above the subterranean cells of the gaol. To

Downriver from Cardigan Bridge

Original gate?: Cardigan Gaol

the rear of Stanley House, originally part of the administrative buildings, the remnants of Nash's circular windows are still in evidence, while a heavily-barred door, strengthened with a formidable bolt, is set into what appears to be the goalyard wall to the north. Cardigan Gaol was sold by the Gaol Commissioners in 1879-80 to Captain William Williams, master mariner, who redeveloped the site and named Stanley House after his wife, Mary Stanley. Mr. Davies, the present owner of Stanley House and a descendant of William Williams, has a portrait of the stern captain and his schooner, the work of John Loos of Antwerp.

Despite claims for the existence of an earlier foundation, documentary evidence for Cardigan Priory first appears in the form of a charter by which Rhys ap Gruffydd, prince of South Wales, granted "the cell of Cardigan and all its appurtenances" to the Benedictine Abbey of St. Peter, Chertsey, sometime after 1165. The priory was located on the north bank of the Teifi near the old Cardigan Bridge spanning the river opposite the west end of St. Mary's Church. The site, enjoying splendid views over the marshland up-river, is now the Memorial Hospital, part of whose basement includes several of the old priory cells. The priory and its handful of English Monks remained under the control of Chertsey until the Dissolution, providing an income of 30 nobles annually arising from tributes paid by pilgrims visiting the much-hallowed shrine of "The Virgin and Taper"[126]. As with a similar figure at Haverfordwest, little is known of the origins of the wooden Cardigan image of the Virgin and Child, the former holding an extinguished taper in her hand. Traditionally the figure was believed to have been found on the banks of the Teifi, the unextinguishable taper having burnt itself out when some miscreant committed the sin of forswearing himself after praying before it. The taper eventually came to be venerated as a relic; an object of pilgrimage and a source of great spiritual strength. In accordance with the prominence given to swearing by relics in the codes of Hywel Dda, pilgrims and others regularly swore their oaths before the taper, for, as Glanmor Williams pointed out, the spiritual power of images of this sort was comparable only with that exercised by the great holy roods[127]. To "Vicar General" Thomas Cromwell and others of Henry VIII's officials such doings were anathema and it was declared on the King's authority that the Prior and Vicar should preach against such "abhominable idolatry" and ". . . arrange or cause to be done away all manner clothes fygured waxe delusyons of myracles shroudes and other entysementes of the ignorante people to pilgrimage and ydolatory"[128]. Presumably Virgin, Child, taper and all met their end at the hands of Cromwell's vandalistic iconoclasts.

In the scramble for the spoils of Dissolution, Cardigan Priory fell firstly to William Cavendish, gentleman usher to Cardinal Wolsey and eventually, by grant of James I, to Francis Philips, whose descendants held the property for several generations. By way of the marriage of James Philips, a colonel in the Parliamentary army, to Katherine Fowler, daughter of a wealthy Puritan merchant of London, Cardigan priory was set on course for a fleeting period of fame as a literary salon under the aegis of Katherine, known to history as "The Matchless Orinda". Admired by Dryden, and later by Keats, "Orinda" passed most of her short life in the Priory before being carried off by smallpox in 1664 at the age of 33[129]. Keenly alive to the pleasures of life, and a cavalier at heart, she nevertheless remained loyal to her husband through the difficult years of the Civil Wars and the settling of accounts which came with the Restoration. The antiquary John Aubrey, who reckoned that she had read the Bible from cover to cover before she was 4 years old, leaves us a less than flattering portrait of "Orinda's" appearance; "Very good-natured; not at all high-minded; pretty fatt; not tall; red pumpled face; wrote out verses in Innes, or Mottoes in windowes in her table-booke"[130]. "Orinda's" verses, the first collection appearing in 1667, are replete with fine language and elaborate imagery. Most of the poems are addressed to her circle of close acquaintances and are concerned with the rejection of what, to her, was a dull and barbarous world, in favour of the fostering of friendship and platonic love[131]. Her feelings for the Priory and the virtues of the idyllic rural existence are expressed in "A Country Life" of 1650:

"Secure in these unenvyed walls
I think not on the state,
And pity no man's case that falls
From his ambition's height . . .
While others revel it in state,
Here I'le contented sit
And think I have as good a fate
As wealth or pompe admitt".

With the passing of the Philips family, Cardigan Priory came into the possession of the Pryses of Gogerddan near Aberystwyth, before being sold to Thomas Johnes the elder, whose son, incidentally, removed the medieval glass from the east window of St. Mary's Church to embellish his ill-fated library at Hafod. Henceforth the property passed through many hands until, in 1915, it was purchased for £4250 and converted into a hospital to commemorate the fallen of the Great War. The hospital continues to thrive and it is interesting that a site nearby

"in territorium leprosorum" (leper's ground) was conveyed in 1573 along with "penpont y klivion". Assuming that "klivion" is a corruption of "cleifion" (invalids) it may be that today's hospital is heir to a tradition of caring for the sick initiated by the Priory of Cardigan eight centuries ago[132].

It is not far from Cardigan bridge to the sea and the River Teifi soon flows into a broad estuary of shifting channels and sandpits, bounded by saltmarsh and dunes. Even today, the brief journey from Cardigan to the sea is fraught with hazards due to the continual movement of underwater sandbanks near the estuary mouth upriver from Cardigan Bar. Elizabethan sailors were well aware of the tricky problems involved in negotiating this stretch of water. As George Owen of Henllys wrote of the Teifi below Cardigan; ". . . before it cometh to the barre it receiveth in a rill at Meynian moore & so to the sea, where the sands raysed by the sea make a discomodiouse and dangerouse barre hindering much of the trade of shipping to these partes of the Countrie"[133].

The final reaches of the river and the estuary itself support a marvellously diverse population of birds. Waders dabble hopefully among the fishing boats on the mudflats; plovers and terns swoop across Poppit beach and legions of small seed-eaters forage busily among the brambles, gorse and ragwort skirting the sand dunes. Since sand dunes attract people and people are inimical to sand dunes, the authorities have seen fit to fence off extensive areas so as to promote dune stabilisation by marram grass planting. Public access is by way of a network of wooden trackways which, even in the appalling summer of 1985, resounded to the clatter of feet as intrepid beach-lovers wandered towards the sand in the forlorn hope that the sun might eventually appear! Some, bedecked in "wet suits", strutted about purposefully with their windsurfers; others, more scantily attired, timorously approached the water's edge while their more sensible brethren huddled with bottles behind multi-coloured windbreaks, pestered by patrolling dogs, crippled by the chill wind and irritated by miserable children.

If the weather is sometimes dreadful there are

The Teifi beyond Cardigan

always the views. Views of the river, awash with pleasure boats, seagulls and waterskiers, of the cornfields sweeping down to the dramatically rocky coastline, and of Cardigan Island lying just off the coast and looking for all the world like a great beached whale. To the south of the estuary, more or less opposite Cardigan Island, the salt-laden wind lashes the bracken-covered flanks of Cemaes Head whose high, scarred cliffs support gulls and choughs and increasing numbers of that most exciting of birds, the peregrine falcon. At sea level, where cormorants skim the water, inaccessible caves provide a relatively secure birthplace for seal pups although even these are not completely proof against the killer whales which occasionally plunder the colony in the winter months.

For the visitor satiated with natural history, there are the diversions of St. Dogmaels (Llandudoch) clinging to the hillside on the south bank of the river. Like other villages and settlements on this coast, St. Dogmaels was regularly visited, for less than friendly purposes, by Norse raiders who put it to the flames and sword and destroyed its ancient Celtic church in 987. Dark

Age St. Dogmaels, then, was not the safest of places in which to live! Perhaps it was the sense of insecurity engendered by constant stress in those remote times which moved Sir Richard Colt Hoare to note, at the end of the 18th century, that "... the inhabitants of St. Dogmaels (a fierce and hardy race) seldom connect themselves with their neighbours but intermarry entirely amongst themselves"[134].

In 1115 this "fierce and hardy race" played host to a dozen monks brought to St. Dogmaels by Robert Fitzmartin of Cemais, one of the principal Norman conquerors of South Wales. These were members of the Tiron Order, founded by St. Bernard of Abbeville (d. 1117) whose particularly austere way of life was based on a rigorous regime of manual labour and strict adherence to the Benedictine rule. By 1120 the early monastery had been elevated to the status of an abbey, endowed with extensive lands in Devon, Pembrokeshire and Wexford, and subsequently with urban properties in St. Dogmaels and Fishguard. The Fitzmartin family were keen for the abbey to be built on a grand scale and, doubtless to promote the name of Fitzmartin along with the greater glory of God, contributed hugely to the enterprise throughout the 12th and 13th centuries. When Archbishop Baldwin and Giraldus Cambrensis were entertained at St. Dogmaels by the Lord Rhys in 1188, the church and monastic structures around the cloister had reached an advanced stage of construction. A century later the abbey was complete, providing, in this remote corner of the realm, a superb example of the splendours of the freely-flowing Early English style [135].

The purity of the ideals of the founders of St. Dogmaels were pursued less than diligently by their successors. As Gascon wine flowed into the port of Cardigan and revenues from the granges swelled the abbey coffers, austerity was swept away by self-indulgence, and mortification of the flesh gave way to the pursuit of worldly pleasures. The report of a Visitation to the abbey in 1401-2 pointed out that a mere three monks were in residence and these were, ". . . consuming the sustenance of a very large number, to the manifest withdrawal of divine worship". Finding that the lay brothers were engaged in "excessive wandering" to taverns and "unlawful places" the Visitors ordered that henceforth no-one associated with the abbey was to go to St. Dogmaels without a very good reason. The monks, it seems, along with all manner of secular people, were wont to assemble in the house of mercy, ". . . not for the sake of contemplation, but of idle gossip together and drinking". To prevent such misdemeanours it was ordered (rather callously), that no fire be lit, "except at the coming of frost and intolerable cold". Noting the homeric drinking habits of the monks, the report recommended a substantial cut in the wine allowance, a recommendation that probably came as a rude shock to Howel Lange, one of the more bibulous of the brethren. He, we are told, ". . . on account of his excess and the evil deeds committed by him . . . shall not drink wine, nor metheglin, on which it has been his habit to get drunk, but he shall give away and distribute his portion of wine to the poor in the abbot's presence" [136].

At the Dissolution an abbot and eight monks

St. Dogmael's Abbey

St. Dogmael's Abbey: detail

held sway at St. Dogmaels assisted by half-a-dozen servants whose wages totalled £3 - 6 - 8. In 1543 the dissolved abbey, its lands and manorial rights fell to John Bradshaw, an ancestor of the regicide, who took little interest in the fabric of the buildings which steadily fell into ruin, the decaying walls being plundered for building stone by local farmers and villagers. Two hundred and fifty years after Bradshaw's succession, the traveller H. P. Wyndham spoke of "... the dirty village of St. Dogmael (sic)", wherein most of the abbey buildings had been converted to private use[137]. Thanks to the efforts of "Cadw", the body responsible for the protection of ancient monuments in Wales, the husk of the abbey is presently preserved and, if only a shadow of its former glory, it still remains a place for quiet contemplation, for which purpose it was originally intended. Meanwhile, oblivious to decay, indifferent to time and untroubled by the affairs of men, the Teifi flows towards the sea ...

Postscript

Dean Swift maintained that there were only three reasons for travelling; imbecility of mind, infirmity of body and inevitable necessity. Given conditions of travel in the early 18th century, this cynical view is easy to understand. After all, the unfortunate Dean, who never enjoyed the best of health, was forever journeying back and forth to Ireland, braving the rigours of the Holyhead crossing, the nerve-shattering nightmare of the stagecoach and the bone-chilling nights in damp and noisome inns. Besides all this, he suffered at the hands of rapacious ferrymen, impudent ostlers and a whole legion of minions who seem to have conspired to make travelling as unpleasant as possible. Even the most jaded modern traveller, put-upon by scandalously overpriced roadside cafes, ghastly self-service petrol stations, and an unspeakable railway system regularly plagued with strike-fever, would agree that, in general, conditions of travel have improved since Swift's time. Our hotels may be less salubrious than those in Europe and elsewhere, our food less varied and our drink less stimulating, yet our countryside remains superb and incomparable. Nowhere in the world is such tremendous variety encompassed in so small a space. Geologically, topographically, architecturally and archaeologically, Britain is a unique gem sparkling wonderfully in the reluctant northern sunlight. And what is more, that gem is there for all to enjoy and cherish.

Travelling may still have its bugbears, but thanks to developments in communications it has ceased, for most of us, to be "an inevitable necessity". Increased affluence (for those who have jobs), increased leisure (for those who have not) and widespread car ownership, has meant that today more people are visiting the countryside in pursuit of pleasure than ever before. To the city dweller car ownership has its drawbacks, including the unwelcome visitations of vandals, the predatory behaviour of traffic wardens and that antisocial and quite un-British device, the wheel clamp. But what a boon the motor-car becomes when it is time to escape the urban sprawl! Once the traveller is belted in behind the wheel, the countryside beckons and the high-rise blocks retreat. This book has been written with such a traveller in mind; to give him a whiff of the landscape of Wales, albeit a tiny portion of that grey-green, hazy, mysterious but hospitable country.

To a limited extent the "traditional" nature of the Welsh landscape persists and a ghostly traveller from the 1880's would have relatively little difficulty in recognising many of the features of that time. Coniferous forests now march darkly across the hills, ugly scars of new farm roads gouge their way around upland slopes, and chemically fed single-species swards have replaced many of the botanically-rich meadows; yet the basic layout of farm and village remains. Within this layout, though, much has changed. The passage of a century has seen the virtual disppearance of the wheelwright, the blacksmith, the cooper, the clog-maker and the multitude of other craftsmen whose skills cemented the organic relationship between village and farm. More recently there has been something of a rebirth of interest in the countryside of history, in part fostered by an in-flow of non-Welsh people who have arrived in the Principality in pursuit of the "good life", peace and quiet and for a variety of other motives. Craft centres, "working" museums, wildlife parks and the like are now widespread but, like the ubiquitous souvenir shop, they cater predominantly for a growing number of tourists. Such enterprises are all very well in themselves, providing diversion for many, employment for a few and perhaps even having a modest impact upon rural education and landscape conservation. But is this enough to stem the apparently inexorable erosion of the rich cultural traditions and even the physical fabric of the Welsh countryside?

The Welsh language is alive and well, thanks to the efforts of those dedicated activists who have lobbied, cajoled and harassed the educational and broadcasting authorities over the years. But in reality language and literature are merely vehicles in which the totality of cultural experience is expressed. The culture of a peasant society, and I use the term "peasant" in its strictest context, arises from a body of tradition, both real and imagined, with roots deeply embedded in the essence of country life, the soil itself. The monumental figures in *The Mabinogion,* the heroes of whom the bards sang at such inordinate length, the litigious squire in his *plas,* all ultimately depended upon the arched back and the sweating brow of the labouring peasant. Work in field and byre provide enduring images in the poetry and prose of Welshmen whether it be written in the old language or in English, while the countryside in all its moods is a dominant theme in any exhibition of Welsh paintings. The landscape, alternately rain-swept and sun-dappled, was the crucible of the culture, an inescapable back-cloth against which those who worked in it told and re-told an extraordinary corpus of folk-tales some of whose origins lay deep in antiquity. Concurrently they created their own myth, for within a society where few people moved far beyond the home hearth unusual local events assumed tremendous significance and with generations of story-telling these became progressively metamorphosed from fact into legend.

But all this is to talk of the past, and I return to the earlier question. What is Wales, and in particular West Wales, doing to nurture and conserve the all-important landscape of the past and to bequeath a countryside which will gain the praise of future generations? Superficially, especially in comparison with many parts of England, all looks well. Rivers like the Teifi flow through pastoral countryside, running past old-established farmsteads, skirting the remains of ancient woodlands and bisecting market towns. Closer scrutiny though, reveals a very different picture. Amalgamation has dramatically reduced the number of smaller farmsteads (and thus the opportunity for young people to gain a foothold on the farming ladder), ancient fieldbanks have been removed and replaced by wire fencing, layered hedges are virtually non-existent, and much natural woodland has been devastated by livestock—all in the interests of profitable farming. No-one would deny the

farmer's right to a living nor his massive contribution to the well-being of the nation over the past half century. But land ownership is a privilege and it is sometimes conveniently forgotten that *duty* marches hand-in-hand with privilege. A fundamentally vital duty is that of passing on to subsequent generations a farmscape both agriculturally productive and environmentally and aesthetically harmonious. Landowners of two centuries ago absolutely understood this duty and laid out their farms, houses and woodland with an almost instinctive feeling for local building materials, topography and aspect, while the man who planted a hundred acres of oak and beech woodlands was thinking less about his own benefit than that of his heirs two or three generations ahead.

Wild upland moors and bleak rock-strewn hillsides have their particular attractions, but so too does a well-managed farmscape—especially where *scale* has been controlled and where management has been sympathetic towards the non-food producing facets of that farmscape. In general, both farmers and landowners of post-War years have failed to respond to the need for landscape and environmental "enhancement", to their own discredit and that of the governments and taxpayers that have encouraged and financed modern farm development. Even if we forget about such things as the neglect of farm woodlands and the destruction of hedgebanks and think only of the shameful desecration of the farmstead itself, it is a depressing picture. Our journey down the Teifi provides ample examples of rusting tin sheds, noisome slurry lagoons, stark, half-finished silage bunkers and concrete and asbestos livestock buildings; unplanned, unsightly and soulless. Minimal attempts seem to have been made to adapt existing buildings to the needs of modern farming practice and any intuitive sense of conservation has given way to the demands of cheapness and convenience. The farmer on the whole has done little to improve the rural environment over the past 40 years. Yet things are gradually changing. Grant aid for food production is being slashed, there is talk of imposing rigorous planning controls on farming, and at last, the agricultural advisory services are coming to pay more attention to the aesthetics of farm building design. With luck, this change of direction, enforced by food surpluses and the pressure of public opinion, will not have come too late. It may not be too late, given the provision of properly-directed financial aid, for farmsteads the length and breadth of Britain to be given a much needed facelift. New buildings need to be sited with extreme care and to be constructed of materials harmonious with the local landscape. Stone and slate are available in abundance in many parts of the country and could be used to advantage for facing and re-roofing existing structures, the labour employed being subsidised with savings from the present unemployment benefit. Besides providing a tremendous stimulus to the rural workforce this sort of measure would go at least part of the way towards developing a farmscape of which we and our successors can be justly proud. A little imagination, a lot of commitment and a widespread rekindling of the idea of responsibility to posterity are all that is required.

If the creation of the future landscape is a grave responsibility, so is the conservation of the landscape of the past. For decades organisations like the Councils for the Protection of Rural England and Wales, the Nature Conservancy Council and the Royal Commission on Ancient Monuments have struggled to heighten public awareness of the deeply serious matter of the disappearance of natural environments and the destruction of ancient monuments. Recent legislation, involving the scheduling of archaeological sites and monuments and the creation of Sites of Special Scientific Interest has gone some way towards stopping the rot, yet the problem remains. Ancient woodlands still shelter livestock, to the detriment of regeneration; field monuments, earthworks and standing stones remain prey to the unwelcome attentions of bulldozers, and historically-important farm buildings, cottages and country houses are disappearing at an alarming rate, as are the remnants of our more recent industrial past. Such are the very heart of our history; organic

links with the past, every bit as important as the manuscripts and documents comfortably nestling in County Records Offices.

The financial and intellectual resources of official conservation bodies *must* be directed first and foremost to conservation *per se* and castles and earthworks must not be allowed to crumble while bureaucrats debate the whys and wherefores. Those monuments currently under state care are admirably served but what is now required is a commitment by local and national authorities to record, protect and conserve the numerous structures not currently under protection.

Conservation, both of historical material and the natural environment, has little to do with sentiment and can be substantiated on sound commercial and biological grounds. The scientist concerned with the breeding of plants and animals will testify to the vital importance of maintaining a broad genetic base in natural populations, while anyone who understands the role of tourism in our economy will know that visitors to Britain are impressed, above all, by the cultural, historical and natural diversity of the countryside. In Britain, and more especially in Wales, the past is physically inescapable and it is virtually impossible to travel more than a mile without passing a mansion, an earthwork, an early church or an ancient field system. How far, one wonders, does this inevitable, and sometimes even oppressive, sense of the omnipresent past account for our long history of social and political stability? Perhaps it is no accident that societies constantly plagued with revolution and *coup d'etat* are often those whose roots were destroyed by colonialisation or whose more recent cultural progress has been directed by the politics of totalitarianism. If indeed a landscape is a condition of the spirit and the history of a people, to paraphrase Gibbon, more than a register of its crimes, follies and misfortunes, then the very survival of our civilised values depends upon the conservation of the tangible evidence of our past. There may just still be time.

Footnotes

[1] L. T. Smith (ed.), *Leland's Itinerary in Wales, 1536-1539*, London, 1906, p. 118.

[2] For a comprehensive review of the history of Welsh woodlands see, W. Linnard, *Welsh Woods and Forests; History and Utilisation*, National Museum of Wales, 1982. Recent official encouragement of the development and conservation of farm woodlands and the ready availability of grant-aid for deciduous tree planting may help to stem the current rot. Indeed, the remarkably successful "Broad-leaved Woodlands Planting Scheme" announced by the Forestry Commission after the completion of this book may yet effect a dramatic increase in the wooded area of Wales and the rest of the United Kingdom.

[3] T. Jones Pierce, Strata Florida Abbey, *Ceredigion*, *I, 1950, passim*. See also D. H. Williams, *The Welsh Cistercians*, Tenby, 1984, pp. 197-212.

[4] J. E. J. Jones, Fairs in Cardiganshire, *Cards, Antiq. Soc. Trans., VII, 1930, passim*.

[5] S. M. Powell, Pilgrim Routes to Strata Florida, *Cards. Antiq. Soc. Trans., VIII, 1931, passim*.

[6] R. J. Colyer, Nanteos; a landed estate in decline, 1800-1930, *Ceredigion, IX(1), 1980*, pp. 56-75.

[7] T. Jones (trans. and ed.), *Brut y Tywysogion or The Chronicle of the Princes*, Cardiff, 1952.

[8] E. R. Horsfall-Turner, *Walks and Wanderings in County Cardigan*, Bingley, 1901, p. 30.

[9] N.L.W. MS. 6703.

[10] In 1898 a group of German chemists had successfully demonstrated the industrial potential of the bog but lack of capital had prevented exploitation. Locally it was believed that if money were to become available, hundreds of people would be employed in the industrial extraction of lubricating oils, ammonia, paraffin and naptha from the peat. *Cardigan and Teifiside Advertiser, September 29, 1911*.

[11] D. Rees, *Tregaron, Historical and Antiquarian*, Llandysul, 1936, *passim*.

[12] H. Lloyd-Johnes, The Lesser County Houses of Cardiganshire, *Ceredigion 2(1), 1953*, p. 5.

[13] R. J. Colyer, *The Welsh Cattle Drovers*, Cardiff, 1976, *passim*.

[14] W. J. Lewis, The condition of labour in mid-Cardiganshire in the early Nineteenth Century, *Ceredigion, 4, 1963*, p. 330.

[15] "Ap Adda", The Stocking Dealer, *The Red Dragon, II, 1882*, pp. 41-43.

[16] J. Hucks, *A Pedestrian Tour through North Wales*, London, 1795, pp. 122-123.

[17] J. Barber, *A Tour through South Wales and Monmouthshire*, London, 1803, p. 123.

[18] N.L.W. Glanpaith MS 344.

[19] Vestry Book of the Parish of Caron.

[20] Or, at least, so claims his tombstone.

[21] N.L.W. Bronwydd MS 299.

[22] E. G. Bowen, *Britain and the Western Seaways*, London, 1972; E. G. Bowen, *Saints, Seaways and Celtic Settlement*, Cardiff, 1967.

[23] *New Catholic Encyclopedia, 11*; E. A. Livingstone (ed.), *The Concise Oxford Dictionary of the Christian Church*, Oxford, 1977; J. W. Jones (ed. and trans.), *Rhigyfarch's Life of St. David*, Cardiff, 1967.

[24] E. G. Bowen, *The St. David of History*, Aberystwyth, 1982, p. 24; G. Gruffydd and H. Parri Owen, The Earliest Mention of St. David?; An Addendum, *Bulletin of the Board of Celtic Studies, XIX, 1962*, pp. 231-2.

[25] N.L.W. Gilbertson MS 17; Lucas MS 1614.

[26] R. O. Jones, Coleg Bek at Llanddewibrefi, *Cards. Antiq. Soc. Trans., XII, 1937, passim*.

[27] G. Williams, *The Welsh Church from Conquest to Reformation*, Cardiff, 1962, *passim*.

[28] J. Willis-Bund (ed.), *The Black Book of St. Davids*, London, 1902, p. 43.

[29] W. J. Lewis, *Leadmining in Wales*, Cardiff, 1967, *passim*.

[30] B. Phillips, *Peterwell; The History of a Mansion and its Infamous Squire*, Llandysul, 1983, p. 1.

[31] *Dictionary of Welsh Biography*.

[32] D. C. Jenkins (ed.), *The Diary of Thomas Jenkins of Llandeilo, 1826-1870*, Dragon Books, 1976, p. 53.

[33] N.L.W., Bishops Transcripts; Pencarreg, 1846.

[34] R. J. Colyer, *Roads and Trackways of Wales*, Moorland, 1984, Ch. 1.

[35] Gwyn Jones and Thomas Jones (trans. and ed.), *The Mabinogion*, Dragons Dream Books, 1982, *passim*.

[36] Notes and Queries, *Cards. Antiq. Soc. Trans. XII. 1937*, p. 35.

[37] D. L. Evans, Rhuddlan Deivi, *Cards. Antiq. Soc. Trans., VII, 1930*, pp. 60-61.

[38] E. G. Bowen, The Teifi Valley as a Religious Frontier, *Ceredigion, VII, 1972*, p. 1.

[39] B. Coppleston-Crow, The Dual Nature of the Irish Colonisation of Dyfed in the Dark Ages, *Studia Celtica, XVI, 1981*, pp. 1-25.

[40] I. T. Hughes, The Background to Llandysul, *Ceredigion, 3, 1956-9, passim*.

[41] Recent scholarly works in this area, containing excellent bibliographies include, G. Guilbert (ed.), *Hill-Fort Studies, Essays for A. H. A. Hogg*, Leicester, 1981; and Richard Bradley, *The Social Foundations of Prehistoric Britain*, Longmans, 1984. Excellent popular works, ideal for the general reader are: Richard Muir, *Riddles in the British Landscape*, London, 1981, and Christopher Taylor, *Village and Farmstead*, George Phillip, 1983.

[42] G. H. Williams and C. J. Delaney, A Celtic Head from Llandysul, *Carm. Antiq., XVIII, 1982, passim*.

[43] H. R. Evans, Llandysul in 1857, *Carm. Antiq., III, 1961, passim*.

[44] I. G. Jones, and D. Williams, *The Religious Census of 1851, A Calendar of Returns relating to Wales, I*, Cardiff, 1976, *passim*.

[45] I. T. Hughes and J. R. Jenkins, The Church of St. Tyssul, Llandysul, *Ceredigion, V, 1964*, pp. 424-436.

[46] N.M.R. files, R.C.A.M. (Wales), Aberystwyth.

[47] H. R. Evans, Llandysul Church; Minute Book of the Vestry and Parish Meetings, *Ceredigion, 1(1), 1950, passim.*

[48] E. Tyrell-Green. Ironwork in the Teifi Valley, *Y Cymmrodor, 40, 1929,* p. 17.

[49] *Commission of Inquiry into South Wales, 1844.*

[50] J. G. Jenkins, *The Welsh Woollen Industry,* Cardiff, 1969; R. Ian Jack, Fulling-mills in Wales and the March before 1547, *Archaeologia Cambrensis, CXXX, 1981, passim.*

[51] J. G. Jenkins, *Dre-fach Felindre and the Woollen Industry,* Llandysul, 1984.

[52] O. T. Jones, The Glacial and Post-glacial History of the Lower Teifi Valley, *Quar. Jour. Geol. Soc., 121, 1965, passim.*

[53] T. Davies, *John Nash, The Prince Regent's Architect,* Newton Abbot, 1973, pp. 27, 28.

[54] R. J. Colyer, The Gentry and the County in nineteenth century Cardiganshire, *Welsh History Review, 10(4), 1981,* pp. 534-535.

[55] P. D. G. Thomas, Jacobitism in Wales, *Welsh History Review, I(1), 1960,* pp. 279-300.

[56] H. M. Colvin (ed.), *History of the King's Works,* H.M.S.O., 1963.

[57] In H. A. Lloyd, *The Gentry of South Wales, 1540-1640,* Cardiff, 1968, pp. 125-126.

[58] D. Williams, *The Rebecca Riots,* Cardiff, 1971, p. 21.

[59] G. H. Jenkins, *Literature, Religion and Society in Wales, 1660-1730,* Cardiff, 1978, *passim.* Rhydderch ap Ieuan Llwyd, Deputy-Justiciar for the county in 1388 and an expert on Welsh legal procedures, may well have patronised the production of copies of the Welsh laws in the Teifi Valley in the late 14th century. (R. A. Griffiths, Gentlemen and Rebels in later Medieval Cardiganshire, *Ceredigion, 5, 1964-7,* pp. 17-25).

[60] *Dictionary of Welsh Biography.* Among others involved in the venture at Adpar were the Makeigs of Cardigan, a Scots family who had settled in the area in the 17th century, Stephen Parry of Noyadd Trefawr (1675-1724), Walter Lloyd of Coedmor, Theophilus Evans of Pen-y-Wenallt (1693-1769) and Jenkin Thomas of Cwmdu (1690-1763) an interesting collection of gentlemen and artisans. (See M. J. Baylis, The Makeigs in Cardigan, *Ceredigion, VII(1), 1972,* pp. 70-74).

[61] J. G. Jenkins, The coracle as a fishing craft on Welsh rivers, in *Folk and Farm; Essays in Honour of A. T. Lucas,* Dublin, 1976, *passim.*

[62] M. W. Thompson, *The Journeys of Sir Richard Colt Hoare through Wales and England, 1793-1810,* Gloucester, 1983, p. 78.

[63] B. H. Malkin, *The Scenery, Antiquities and Biography of South Wales,* London, 1804, p. 437.

[64] *Bye-gones Relating to Wales and Monmouthshire,* 1876.

[65] J. Evans, *Letters written through ... South Wales,* London, 1805, p. 78.

[66] S. R. Meyrick, *History and Antiquities of the County of Cardigan,* London, 1888, p. 163.

[67] *Cardigan and Teifiside Advertiser,* June 3rd, 1966.

[68] M. Rhys (ed.), *Minister's Accounts for West Wales, 1277-1306,* London, 1936.

[69] R. J. Colyer, Some aspects of land occupation in Nine-teenth Century Cardiganshire, *Trans. Hon. Soc. Cymm., 1981,* p. 82.

[70] A. H. A. Hogg and D. J. C. King, Early Castles in Wales: a preliminary list, *Archaeologia Cambrensis, CXII, 1963.*

[71] *Brut y Tywysogion, op. cit.,* p.p. 26-30.

[72] J. G. Jenkins, Bowl Turners and Spoon Carvers, *Folk Life, I, 1963,* p.p. 35-40.

[73] H. M. Vaughan, *The South Wales Squires,* London, 1926, p. 33.

[74] Anon., *A Short History of the Tivyside Hunt, 1736-1939* (Dyfed R.O., DX/13/3).

[75] Vaughan, *op. cit.,* p. 41.

[76] N.L.W. Noyadd Trefawr MS 1806.

[77] Dyfed R.O. D/LL/617.

[78] Dyfed R.O. D/LL/618.

[79] Dyfed R.O. D/LL/619; D/LL/622.

[80] Dyfed R.O. D/LL/620-7.

[81] Dyfed R.O. D/LL/2311.

[82] J. R. Phillips, *The History of Cilgerran,* London, 1867, pp. 138-143.

[83] R. Warner, *A Second Walk through Wales,* London, 1789, *passim.*

[84] The forge had been purchased in 1751 by Walter Lloyd of Coedmor from John Symmons of Llanstinan in Pembrokeshire for £63 (Dyfed RO D/LL/232).

[85] Dyfed R.O. D/LL/240.

[86] M. Evans, *Coedmore Forge, Llechryd,* in T. Barnes and N. Yates (eds.), *Carmarthenshire Studies,* Carmarthen, 1974.

[87] J. G. Jenkins, Fish Weirs and Traps, *Folk Life, 12, 1974,* p. 5.

[88] Dyfed R. O. D/LL/629.

[89] Dyfed R.O. D/LL/630.

[90] Dyfed R.O. D/LL/469.

[91] Dyfed R.O. D/LL/2694.

[92] Dyfed R.O. D/LL/682.

[93] Dyfed R.O. D/LL/863.

[94] Williams, (Rebecca Riots), *op. cit.,* p. 225.

[95] *Cardigan and Teifiside Advertiser,* June 23, 1933.

[96] D. Williams and I. G. Jones (eds.), *The Religious Census of 1851, A Calendar of Returns relating to Wales, I,* Cardiff, 1976.

[97] T. W. Barker, *Particulars relating to endowments in the Diocese of St. Davids, III,* Carmarthen, 1907, pp. 162-3.

[98] Dyfed R.O. D/LL/2226.

[99] Phillips, (Cilgerran), *op. cit.,* pp. 165-7.

[100] J. G. Jenkins, The Maritime Heritage of some southern Ceredigion villages, *Ceredigion, IX, 1982, passim.*

[101] N.L.W. MS 55350.

[102] Dyfed R.O. D/LL/469.

[103] R. A. Griffiths, *The Principality of Wales in the later Middle Ages,* Cardiff, 1972, pp. 306-17.

[104] N.L.W. Noyadd Trefawr MS 419.

[105] N.L.W. Edwinsford MS 3198.

[106] N.L.W. Tyllwyd MS 301.

[107] I.G. Sanders, Trade and Industry in Cardiganshire Towns in the Middle Ages, *Ceredigion, 3, 1956,* pp. 332-3.

[108] Dyfed R.O. D/LL/489.

[109] Phillips (Cilgerran) *op. cit.,* pp. 46-7.

[110] Evans, (South Wales), *op. cit.*, p. 320.

[111] *Cilgerran Castle*, H.M.S.O., Cardiff, 1957, *passim*.

[112] *Cardigan and Teifiside Advertiser*, October 16th, 1874.

[113] *Cardigan and Teifiside Advertiser*, October 20th, 1916; June 1st, 1917. Since the completion of this book Coedmor has been purchased from the Lloyd family and is currently being restored.

[114] J. Cule, Thomas Phaer, M.D., of Cilgerran (1510?-1560), *Trans. Hon. Soc. Cymm., 1979, passim*.

[115] E. A. Lewis, The Port Books of the Port of Cardigan in Elizabethan and Stuart Times, *Cards. Antiq. Soc. Trans.*, VII, 1930, *passim*.

[116] N.L.W. Noyadd Trefawr MS 1672.

[117] N.L.W. Bronwydd MS 3370.

[118] Evans, (South Wales), *op. cit.*, pp. 315-6.

[119] J. G. Jenkins, *Maritime Heritage; The Ships and Seamen of Southern Ceredigion*, Gomer, Llandysul, 1982 *passim*.

[120] N.L.W. Morgan Richardson MS 2102.

[121] *Idem*.

[122] Dyfed R.O. D/LL/152.

[123] G. Lipscomb, *Journey into South Wales*, London, 1802, p. 174.

[124] Malkin, *op. cit.*, p. 408.

[125] N.L.W. Kyle MS 51.

[126] S. M. Harris, *Welsh Saints and Shrines, No. 2; Our Lady of Cardigan*, 1964, *passim*. I am grateful to Father Conane of Cardigan for drawing my attention to this and other sources regarding Our Lady of Cardigan.

[127] G. Williams, *op. cit.*, p. 491.

[128] E. M. Pritchard, *Cardigan Priory in the Olden Days*, London, 1904, p. 72.

[129] P. W. Souers, *The Matchless Orinda*, Cambridge, 1931, *passim*.

[130] O. Lawson Dick (ed.), *Aubrey's Brief Lives*, London, 1960, p. 242.

[131] P. H. B. Thomas, *An Edition of the Poems and Letters of Katherine Philips, 1632-1664*, Ph.D. (Wales) thesis, 1982.

[132] N.L.W. Noyadd Trefawr MS 9.

[133] H. Owen (ed.), George Owen, *The Description of Pembrokeshire*, London, 1892, p. 102.

[134] Thompson (Colt Hoare), *op. cit.*, p. 42.

[135] *St. Dogmaels Abbey*, H.M.S.O., London, 1978.

[136] *The Episcopal Register of St. Davids, 1398-1518*, London, 1917, pp. 247-51.

[137] H. P. Wyndham, *A Tour through Wales*, London, 1794, p. 95.

Bibliography

Anon, *A Short History of the Tivyside Hunt, 1736-1939* (Dyfed R.O., DX/13/3).

"Ap Adda", The Stocking Dealer, *The Red Dragon, II, 1882.*

Barber, J., *A Tour through South Wales and Monmouthshire,* London, 1803.

Baylis, M. J., The Makeigs in Cardigan, *Ceredigion, VII(1), 1972.*

Barker, T. W., *Particulars relating to endowments in the Diocese of St. Davids, III,* Carmarthen, 1907.

Bowen, E. G., *Britain and the Western Seaways,* London, 1972.

Ibid., *Saints, Seaways and Celtic Settlement,* Cardiff, 1967.

Ibid., *The St. David of History,* Aberystwyth, 1982.

Ibid., *The Teifi Valley as a Religious Frontier, Ceredigion, VII(1), 1972.*

Bradley, R., *The Social Foundations of Prehistoric Britain,* Longmans, 1984.

Bye-gones relating to Wales and Monmouthshire, 1876.

Cardigan and Teifiside Advertiser.

Cilgerran Castle, H.M.S.O., 1957.

Colvin, H. M., (ed.), *History of the King's Works,* H.M.S.O., 1963.

Commission of Inquiry into South Wales, 1844.

Colyer, R. J., *The Welsh Cattle Drovers,* Cardiff, 1976.

Ibid., *Roads and Trackways of Wales,* Moorland, 1984.

Ibid., The Gentry and the County in nineteenth century Cardiganshire, *Welsh History Review, 10(4), 1981.*

Ibid., Some Aspects of Land Occupation in nineteenth century Cardiganshire, *Trans. Hon. Soc. Cymm., 1981.*

Ibid., Nanteos; a landed estate in decline, 1800-1930, *Ceredigion, IX(1), 1980.*

Coppleston-Crow, B., The Dual Nature of the Irish Colonisation of Dyfed in the Dark Ages, *Studia Celtica, XVI, 1981.*

Cule, J., Thomas Phaer, M.D., of Cilgerran (1510?-1560), *Trans. Hon. Soc. Cymm., 1979.*

Davies, T., *John Nash, The Prince Regent's Architect,* Newton Abbot, 1973.

Dick, O. Lawson, (ed.), *Aubrey's Brief Lives,* London, 1960.

Dictionary of Welsh Biography.

Evans, D. C., Rhuddlan Deivi, *Cards. Antiq. Soc. Trans., VII, 1930.*

Evans, H. R., Llandysul in 1857, *Carmarthen Antiquary, III, 1961.*

Ibid., Llandysul Church; Minutes Book of the Vestry and Parish, *Ceredigion I(1), 1950.*

Evans, J., *Letters Written through . . . South Wales,* London, 1805.

Evans, M., Coedmore Forge, Llechryd, in T. Barnes and N. Yates, (eds.), *Carmarthenshire Studies,* Carmarthen, 1974.

Griffiths, R. A., Gentlemen and Rebels in later Medieval Cardiganshire, *Ceredigion, V, 1964.*

Ibid., *The Principality of Wales in the later Middle Ages,* Cardiff, 1972.

Gruffydd, G., and Owen, H. Parri, The Earliest mention of St. David?; An Addendum, *Bulletin of the Board of Celtic Studies, XIX, 1962.*

Guilbert, G. (ed.), *Hill-Fort Studies, Essays for A. H. A. Hogg,* Leicester, 1981.

Harris, S. M., *Welsh Saints and Shrines, No. 2, Our Lady of Cardigan,* 1964.

Hogg, A. H. A., and King, D. J. C., Early Castles in Wales: a preliminary list, *Archaeologia Cambrensis, CXII, 1963.*

Horsfall-Turner, E. R., *Walks and Wanderings in County Cardigan,* Bingley, 1901.

Hucks, J., *A Pedestrian Tour through North Wales,* London, 1795.

Hughes, I. T., The Background to Llandysul, *Ceredigion, III, 1956.*

Hughes, I. T., and Jenkins, J. R., The Church of St. Tyssul, Llandysul, *Ceredigion, V, 1964.*

Jack, R. I., Fulling Mills in Wales and the March before 1547, *Archaeologia Cambrensis, CXXX, 1981.*

Jenkins, D. C., *The Diary of Thomas Jenkins of Llandeilo, 1826-1870,* Dragon Books, 1976.

Jenkins, G. H., *Literature, Religion and Society in Wales, 1660-1730,* Cardiff, 1978.

Jenkins, J. G., *Maritime Heritage; The Ships and Seamen of Southern Ceredigion,* Llandysul, 1982.

Ibid., *Dre-fach Felindre and the Woollen Industry,* Llandysul, 1984.

Ibid., *The Welsh Woollen Industry,* Cardiff, 1969.

Ibid., Bowl Turners and Spoon Carvers, *Folk Life, I, 1963.*